1st EDITION

Perspectives on Modern World History

Little Rock Nine

1st EDITION

Perspectives on Modern World History

Little Rock Nine

Diane Andrews Henningfeld

Editor

GREENHAVEN PRESS
A part of Gale, Cengage Learning

GALE
CENGAGE Learning·

Farmington Hills, Mich • San Francisco • New York • Waterville, Maine
Meriden. Conn • Mason. Ohio • Chicago

GALE
CENGAGE Learning·

Elizabeth Des Chenes, *Director, Content Strategy*
Cynthia Sanner, *Publisher*
Douglas Dentino, *Manager, New Product*

WCN: 01-100-101

For product information and technology assistance, contact us at
Gale Customer Support, 1-800-877-4253.

For permission to use material from this text or product, submit all requests online at
www.cengage.com/permissions.

Further permissions questions can be e-mailed to permissionrequest@cengage.com.

Articles in Greenhaven Press anthologies are often edited for length to meet page requirements. In addition, original titles of these works are changed to clearly present the main thesis and to explicitly indicate the author's opinion. Every effort is made to ensure that Greenhaven Press accurately reflects the original intent of the authors. Every effort has been made to trace the owners of copyrighted material.

Cover images © Bettmann/Corbis, and © Everett Collection/Alamy.

LIBRARY OF CONGRESS CATALOGING-IN-PUBLICATION DATA

Little Rock Nine / Diane Andrews Henningfeld, book editor.
    pages cm. -- (Perspectives on modern world history)
    Includes bibliographical references and index.
    ISBN 978-0-7377-6368-3 (hardcover)
    1. School integration--Arkansas--Little Rock--History--20th century. 2. African American students --Arkansas--Little Rock--History--20th century. 3. Central High School (Little Rock, Ark.)--History. 4. Little Rock (Ark.)--Race relations. I. Henningfeld, Diane Andrews, editor of compilation.
    LC214.23.L56L58 2014
    379.2'630976773--dc23
                                                              2013034609

Printed in the United States of America
1 2 3 4 5 6 7 18 17 16 15 14

CONTENTS

The Supreme Court rules that the Arkansas law passed in emergency session violates the constitutional rights of African American children and that the Arkansas governor and legislature must abide by federal law concerning the integration of public schools.

CHAPTER 2   **Controversies Surrounding the Little Rock Nine Crisis**

The Nation

The editors of *The Nation* magazine contend that the Constitution gives the president of the United States the right and the obligation to uphold the authority of the federal courts. The editors argue that President Eisenhower must respond to the Arkansas disregard of federal law by sending in troops to enforce laws passed by Congress as interpreted by the Supreme Court of the United States.

R. Carter Pittman

An attorney argues that although the Constitution provides circumstances under which the president of the United States may call out federal troops, those circumstances did not exist in Little Rock, Arkansas. Consequently, the author maintains, the President's use of federal troops was illegal and constituted an invasion of the state of Arkansas.

on white boys and calling a girl "white trash" remembers her experiences during the difficult days from 1957 to 1958.

FOREWORD

"History cannot give us a program for the future, but it can give us a fuller understanding of ourselves, and of our common humanity, so that we can better face the future."

—Robert Penn Warren,
American poet and novelist

The history of each nation is punctuated by momentous events that represent turning points for that nation, with an impact felt far beyond its borders. These events—displaying the full range of human capabilities, from violence, greed, and ignorance to heroism, courage, and strength—are nearly always complicated and multifaceted. Any student of history faces the challenge of grasping the many strands that constitute such world-changing events as wars, social movements, and environmental disasters. But understanding these significant historic events can be enhanced by exposure to a variety of perspectives, whether of people involved intimately or of ones observing from a distance of miles or years. Understanding can also be increased by learning about the controversies surrounding such events and exploring hot-button issues from multiple angles. Finally, true understanding of important historic events involves knowledge of the events' human impact—of the ways such events affected people in their everyday lives—all over the world.

Perspectives on Modern World History examines global historic events from the twentieth century onward by presenting analysis and observation from numerous vantage points. Each volume offers high school, early college level, and general interest readers a thematically arranged anthology of previously published materials that address a major historical event, with an emphasis on international coverage. Each volume opens with background information on the event, then presents the controversies surrounding that event, and concludes with first-person narratives from people who lived through the event or were affected by it. By providing primary sources from the time of the event, as well as relevant commentary surrounding the event, this series can be used to inform debate, help develop critical thinking skills, increase global awareness, and enhance an understanding of international perspectives on history.

Material in each volume is selected from a diverse range of sources, including journals, magazines, newspapers, nonfiction books, personal narratives, speeches, congressional testimony, government documents, pamphlets, organization newsletters, and position papers. Articles taken from these sources are carefully edited and introduced to provide context and background. Each volume of Perspectives on Modern World History includes an array of views on events of global significance. Much of the material comes from international sources and from US sources that provide extensive international coverage.

Each volume in the Perspectives on Modern World History series also includes:

- A full-color **world map**, offering context and geographic perspective.

- An annotated **table of contents** that provides a brief summary of each essay in the volume.

- An **introduction** specific to the volume topic.

- For each viewpoint, a brief **introduction** that has notes about the author and source of the viewpoint, and that provides a summary of its main points.

- Full-color **charts**, **graphs**, **maps**, and other visual representations.

- Informational **sidebars** that explore the lives of key individuals, give background on historical events, or explain scientific or technical concepts.

- A **glossary** that defines key terms, as needed.

- A **chronology** of important dates preceding, during, and immediately following the event.

- A **bibliography** of additional books, periodicals, and websites for further research.

- A comprehensive **subject index** that offers access to people, places, and events cited in the text.

Perspectives on Modern World History is designed for a broad spectrum of readers who want to learn more about not only history but also current events, political science, government, international relations, and sociology—students doing research for class assignments or debates, teachers and faculty seeking to supplement course materials, and others wanting to improve their understanding of history. Each volume of Perspectives on Modern World History is designed to illuminate a complicated event, to spark debate, and to show the human perspective behind the world's most significant happenings of recent decades.

INTRODUCTION

On May 17, 1954, the US Supreme Court ruled on one of the most important and influential cases ever to appear before that body. The case, *Brown v. Board of Education of Topeka*, forever changed the face of public education in the United States. The justices unanimously declared in their ruling that public schools could no longer be segregated. In so doing, the court overturned the long-standing precedent of the 1896 *Plessy v. Ferguson* decision, which stated that the racial segregation of public facilities, including schools, was legal so long as "separate but equal" facilities were provided for both African American and white people.

In practice, the separate but equal policy was anything but equal. Facilities and schools designated for African Americans were generally in disrepair, outdated, and far inferior to those facilities designated for white people. Consequently, beginning in the 1930s, the National Association for the Advancement of Colored People (NAACP) began bringing various suits against corporations, educational institutions, and public facilities that practiced segregation. They argued that segregation was a violation of the Fourteenth Amendment of the United States guaranteeing equal protection under the law.

It took until the 1950s before the NAACP met with success. In June 1950, in *Henderson v. United States*, the court struck down the railway's use of segregated dining cars. Several other cases brought against the University of Oklahoma and the University of Texas for failure to provide equal law education to African Americans also met with success. According to Melvin I. Urofsky, writing in *Black, White, and Brown: The Landmark School Desegregation Case in Retrospect*, "The NAACP would now attack the *Plessy* doctrine frontally, by massing overwhelming evidence to show that separate education could never be truly equal."

In 1951 thirteen parents filed a class action lawsuit against the Topeka, Kansas, school board on behalf of their children, who were denied enrollment at their neighborhood elementary schools because of their race. The District Court ruled in favor of the school board. In 1953 the case made its way to the Supreme Court. At its first hearing, the case remained undecided, and the court asked to rehear the case in late 1953. In September 1953, President Dwight D. Eisenhower appointed Earl Warren as chief justice of the Supreme Court, and it was Warren who led the justices to a unanimous reversal of the District Court's ruling. Voicing the unanimous opinion of the court, Warren stated:

> Segregation of white and Negro children in the public schools of a State solely on the basis of race, pursuant to state laws permitting or requiring such segregation, denies to Negro children the equal protection of the laws guaranteed by the Fourteenth Amendment—even though the physical facilities and other "tangible" factors of white and Negro schools may be equal.

With this ruling, the Court declared that the segregation of public schools was unconstitutional in that it violated the Fourteenth Amendment.

The results of the *Brown v. Board of Education* case had deep ramifications across the country—nowhere more so than in Little Rock, Arkansas. Change was on the way; and as a result, the Little Rock School Board agreed in 1955 that it would develop a plan to slowly integrate Little Rock's schools, beginning with the high school. The plan, as formulated by Superintendent Virgil Blossom, called for integration to occur over six years. The NAACP was not happy with this solution, calling for immediate action. In January 1956, a group of African

American students attempted to enroll in a formerly white school, but were denied admission. The NCAAP brought suit on behalf of the students, but the suit was dismissed and the dismissal later upheld. The school board's gradual integration plan was sufficient, according to the judges.

In the spring of 1957, however, movement toward integration began in earnest. Superintendent Blossom and the school board interviewed eighty African American students who lived in the all-white Central High School district and who showed an interest in attending Central. Of these eighty, Blossom selected seventeen to be the first students to integrate Little Rock schools. Eight of these students, however, dropped out of the process before September, leaving nine students: Melba Pattillo, Minnijean Brown, Elizabeth Eckford, Ernest Green, Gloria Ray, Carlotta Walls, Terrence Roberts, Jefferson Thomas, and Thelma Mothershed. Soon to be called "The Little Rock Nine," these young people were at the center of the crisis watched by the entire nation.

Over the summer of 1957, white citizens who opposed desegregation organized themselves into the Capital Citizens Council and the Mother's League of Central High School. They vowed to prevent the entry of the Little Rock Nine into Central High. In response to the threat of violence at the opening of school, Arkansas governor Orval Faubus called out the Arkansas National Guard to keep the peace and protect citizens. In her memoir *A Mighty Long Way*, Little Rock Nine member Carlotta Walls LaNier recalls her reaction to the National Guard presence: "I honestly believed that I was included in those whom our governor had deployed the Arkansas National Guard to protect. It was shocking to think that a military unit might be necessary to keep the peace on my first day at Central, but I still wanted to go."

On the morning of September 4, 1957, the Little Rock Nine attempted to enter Central High. The National

Guard, to the dismay of the African American students, turned them away. Eckford, not realizing the other students were meeting to go to Central as a group, walked alone to the high school and was quickly surrounded by a mob hurling obscenities at her. The students tried again on September 20 to enter the school, but again, a white mob assembled, and the students were led out of the school under police protection. On September 24, a frustrated and angry Eisenhower sent the 101st Airborne Division of the US Army to Little Rock and nationalized the Arkansas National Guard, placing them under federal, not state, command. By September 25, the Little Rock Nine were finally able to begin their studies at Central High School.

Although the students were admitted to the school, the year ahead was one of suffering and trauma. According to the August 30, 2007, *USA Today*, "The black students were cursed at, jostled and spat upon. Their lockers were broken into; glue was put on their chairs. They got threatening phone calls at home and their families' businesses were boycotted." One student, taunted to the breaking point, dropped a bowl of chili on the offending white student and was subsequently expelled. However, although the year was difficult and despite the legal wrangling that continued for another year, the students succeeded in breaking the color barrier in Little Rock schools.

Little Rock schools were closed during the 1958–1959 school year as Arkansas politicians continued to fight integration. For some, the objection was to federal intervention in what they viewed as a state's right. For others, however, the objection was purely on racial grounds.

Little Rock's schools were opened in 1960, but it took until the 1970s for all grades to be fully integrated. In 1999 the members of the Little Rock Nine were awarded a Congressional Gold Medal for their bravery and courage in the fight for civil rights. Today Central High School is a National Historic Site, the only national park within a functioning public school. Central High and the Central High Museum welcome visitors from around the world to learn about the Little Rock Nine's encounter with history. *Perspectives in Modern World History: Little Rock Nine* examines the historical background surrounding the Little Rock Nine crisis and its impact on the US education system.

World Map

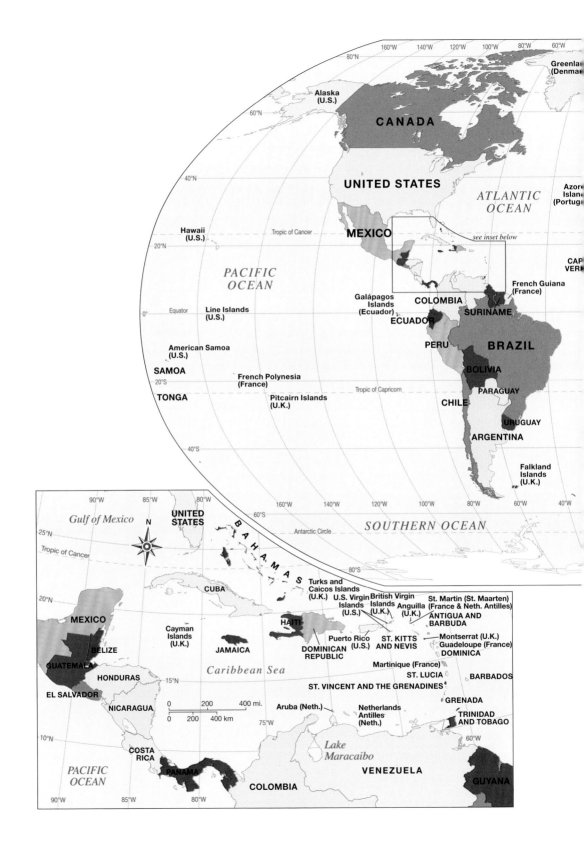

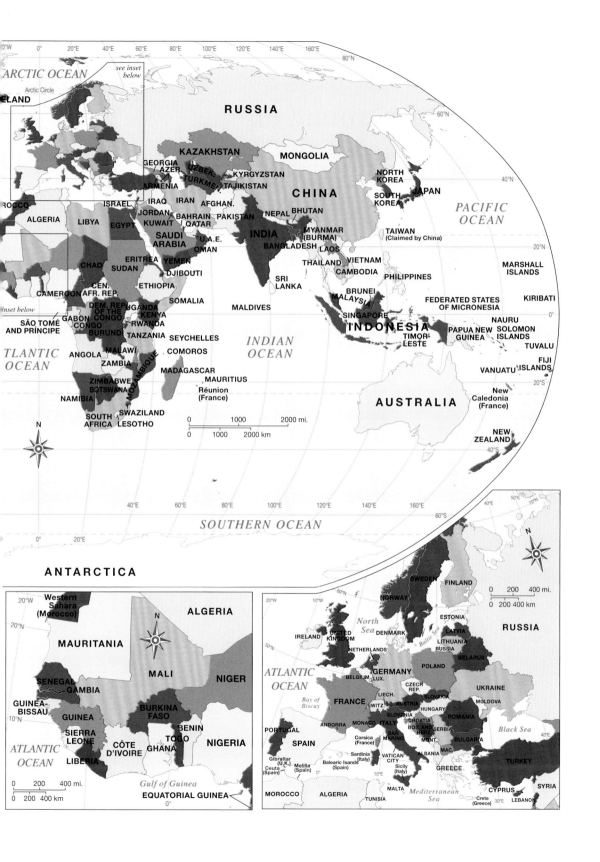

CHAPTER 1

Historical Background on the Little Rock Nine Crisis

Nine Students Fight for School Integration in Little Rock, Arkansas

National Park Service

In the following viewpoint, writers from the National Park Service's Little Rock Central High School National Historic Site supply an overview of the events that led up to the Little Rock Nine crisis. In September 1957, nine African Americans voluntarily transferred to the all-white Central High School in Little Rock, Arkansas. Their actions were in compliance with the 1954 US Supreme Court ruling in the *Brown v. Board of Education of Topeka* case stipulating that all school boards must desegregate public schools. The students were met with violence and racial slurs; despite this, they persevered and their actions form an iconic moment in the history of civil rights in the United States.

Photo on previous page: Elizabeth Eckford (center) is followed by an anti-integration mob after being turned away from Central High School in Little Rock, Arkansas, by National Guardsmen on September 4, 1957. (© Francis Miller/ Time & Life Pictures/ Getty Images.)

Events in the fall of 1957 drew international attention as Little Rock became the epitome of state resistance when Arkansas Governor Orval E. Faubus directly questioned the sanctity of the federal court system and the authority of the Supreme Court's desegregation ruling when nine African-American high school students sought an education at Little Rock Central High School.

The controversy in Little Rock was the first fundamental test of the United States' resolve to enforce African-American civil rights in the face of massive southern defiance during the period following the *Brown* decisions [a US Supreme Court case decision ruling that the racial segregation of public schools is unconstitutional]. When President Dwight D. Eisenhower was compelled by white mob violence to use federal troops to ensure the rights of African-American children to attend the previously all-white Little Rock Central High School, he became the first president since the post-Civil War Reconstruction period to use federal troops in support of African-American civil rights. As a result, the eyes of the world were focused on Little Rock in 1957 and the struggle became a symbol of southern racist reaction, as Governor Faubus created a constitutional crisis.

The Supreme Court Rules on Segregation

On May 17, 1954, the United States Supreme Court ruled that racial segregation in public schools was unconstitutional. In August of 1954, the National Association for the Advancement of Colored People (NAACP) petitioned the Little Rock School Board for immediate integration of the schools. In response, the school board stated that "until the Supreme Court of the United States makes its decision . . . more specific, Little Rock School District will continue with its present program." With this statement, the school board ensured that they would not desegregate the schools of the city quickly. The NAACP (led by lawyer Wiley Branton) petitioned the school board "to take immediate steps to reorganize the public schools under your jurisdiction in accordance with the constitutional principles enunciated by the Supreme Court."

In 1955, responding to further Supreme Court rulings and re-argument of the *Brown v. Board* case, the Little Rock School Board adopted a plan of gradual integration called the Blossom Plan (named for the Little Rock School District superintendent, Virgil T. Blossom). It called for desegregation to begin at the high school level in September of 1957. Lower grades would be gradually integrated over the following six years.

> In 1956 . . . 27 African-American students attempted to register in white Little Rock schools, but were turned down.

While the local, state, and federal governments were trying to figure out ways to desegregate schools, a group of segregationists formed and called themselves the Capital Citizens Council. Their goal was to keep the schools of Little Rock segregated. Another group, headed by several women, formed the Mother's League of Central High School to oppose desegregation.

Fighting Desegregation

The first test came in 1956, when 27 African-American students attempted to register in white Little Rock schools, but were turned down. Instead, they were told to attend school in the newly opened Horace Mann High School for black students at the former Dunbar High School building because construction was not yet completed. Superintendent Blossom assured the student's parents that he wanted to be "kind" to these students, but one NAACP representative said that the superintendent's actions were "more like the old run-around deception, than an honest and conscientious plan of the school board to integrate the schools." Next, the NAACP filed a lawsuit on behalf of 33 black students who were denied admittance to white Little Rock schools in 1956. In *Aaron v. Cooper*, the NAACP stated that their objective in filing the suit "was to secure the prompt and orderly end of segregation in the public schools. We want all children, regardless of race, to have the opportunity to go to the public schools nearest their homes." The suit was dismissed and a federal judge declared that the Little Rock school board acted in "good faith" but the judge retained jurisdiction over the case.

As desegregation of Little Rock schools grew closer, the Arkansas State Legislature approved four "segregation bills" in early 1957. These bills created the State Sovereignty Committee (House Bill 322) to investigate those encouraging integration, removed the mandatory school attendance requirement at all integrated schools (HB 323), required the registration of certain individuals and organizations such as the NAACP (HB 324), and authorized school boards to use school funds to fight integration (HB 325). In addition, the legislature also placed a three percent sales tax on the election ballot to ensure that more money would be spent toward education and fighting desegregation.

The Capital Citizens Council issued a statement in mid-1957 that supported segregation: "The Negroes have ample and fine schools here and there is no need for this problem except to satisfy the aims of a few white and Negro revolutionaries in the local Urban League and the National Association for the Advancement of Colored People."

Other members of the Capital Citizens Council gathered in the summer of 1957 to plan their fight against desegregation. They ran advertisements in newspapers that included the following questions: "At social functions would black males and white females dance together? Would black students join clubs and travel with whites?

Would black and white students use the same rest rooms?"

Growing Turmoil in Arkansas

In the midst of growing turmoil in August 1957, the governor of Georgia came to Arkansas and held a state-wide meeting to oppose desegregation. He praised the Arkansans who were fighting to preserve the right of the state to oppose the federal government (also called state's rights). He also met with the Capital Citizens Council and Governor Faubus to show his support for their efforts.

On the morning of September 2, 1957, Governor Faubus ordered the Arkansas National Guard to prevent nine African-American students from entering Little Rock Central High School. In a televised speech, he proclaimed that it was to prevent violence and protect the students. The nine students were told by the Little Rock school board members to stay away from school for their own safety because the governor had heard a rumor that white supremacists were headed toward Little Rock.

On September 3, 1957, the Mother's League held a sunrise service at Little Rock Central High School. It was attended by members of the Capital Citizens Council, angry parents of white students, and local religious figures. The crowd sang "Dixie," flew the Confederate battle flag, and praised Governor Faubus. Despite the protest, federal Judge Richard Davies issued his ruling that desegregation would continue the next day. In response, Governor Faubus ordered the National Guard to stay at the school.

> Nine black students attempted to enter Little Rock Central High School and were turned away by the National Guard on September 4 [1957].

The nine black students attempted to enter Little Rock Central High School and were turned away by the National Guard on September 4. Ernest Green, Elizabeth Eckford, and Terrence Roberts arrived at the school without their parents. Eckford found herself surrounded by an angry mob. She sat alone on a bus stop bench and waited to go to her mother's work. Later, Eckford remembered, "I tried to see a friendly face somewhere in the mob—someone who maybe would help. I looked into the face of an old woman and it seemed a kind face, but when I looked at her again, she spat on me." At least one sympathetic member of the crowd, Dr. Benjamin Fine, a white reporter from New York, sat down beside her and said, "Don't let them see you cry." The following day, none of the nine students attempted to re-enter the school and the Little Rock School Board requested that desegregation be temporarily halted.

> White students had mixed reactions to the nine African-American students.

In the following days, Governor Faubus appeared on national television to reaffirm his belief in segregation. He also met with President Eisenhower and "assured the President of my desire to cooperate with him in carrying out the duties resting upon both of us under the Federal Constitution." Meanwhile, Judge Davies began legal proceedings against the governor and several National Guardsmen for interfering with integration. Under federal court order, Governor Faubus removed the troops, left the state for a governor's conference, and the city police had to try and keep order at the school.

The Little Rock Nine Enter Central High

Finally, on September 23, the nine African-American students (after facing a crowd of over 1,000 white protestors), entered Little Rock Central High School.

The Little Rock Nine

Melba Pattillo Beals (1941–)
Minnijean Brown (1941–)
Elizabeth Eckford (1941–)
Ernest Green (1941–)
Gloria Cecelia Ray Karlmark (1942–)
Carlotta Walls LaNier (1942–)
Terrence Roberts (1941–)
Jefferson Thomas (1942–2010)
Thelma Mothershed Wair (1940–)

An anonymous man commented, "They've gone in. . . . Oh, God, [they] are in the school." Melba Pattillo Beals, one of the nine, remembered the moment, "I had long dreamed of entering Central High. I could not have imagined what that privilege could cost me."

White students had mixed reactions to the nine African-American students. Several jumped out of windows to avoid contact with the students. Others, like Robin Woods, said, "That was the first time I'd ever gone to school with a Negro, and it didn't hurt a bit."

Outside of the school, black journalists who covered the story were harassed and physically attacked. They ran from the mob and took refuge elsewhere in Little Rock. President Eisenhower was "disgusted" when he heard about the rioting and ordered in federal troops to contain the chaos. Over 1,000 members of the U.S. Army's 101st Airborne Division ("Screaming Eagles") from Fort Campbell, Kentucky, came to Little Rock. The Arkansas National Guard troops at the school were then placed under their command. Observing the soldiers, activist and mentor to the nine students, Daisy Gatson Bates commented that "any time it takes eleven thousand five

THE LITTLE ROCK NINE

hundred soldiers to assure nine Negro children their constitutional rights in a democratic society, I can't be happy."

On September 25, the nine students were escorted back into Central High School after General Edwin

Walker of the United States Army addressed the white students of Little Rock Central High School in the auditorium, "You have nothing to fear from my soldiers, and no one will interfere with your coming, going, or your peaceful pursuit of your studies." When they arrived, the student body reaction was once again mixed. One student commented that "if parents would just go home and let us alone, we'll be all right . . . we just want them to leave us be. We can do it."

The Governor Fights Back

Governor Faubus, meanwhile, took a siege mentality to forced integration at Little Rock Central High School and said, "We are now in occupied territory. Evidence of the naked force of the federal government is here apparent, in these, unsheathed bayonets in the backs of schoolgirls." After less than a month at the school, most members of the 101st Airborne left Arkansas and turned their duties over to the Arkansas National Guard, which was now federalized. Discipline problems resurfaced at the school after the federal troops left and school records indicate that incidents of harassment of the nine students escalated.

Local business leaders, who had called for peaceful compliance with court orders for school integration, were met with resistance. For instance, the Mother's League sought through the court system to have the federal troops removed from Central High School on the grounds that it violated federal and state constitutions (the action was dismissed) and Governor Faubus issued statements expressing his desire that the nine students be removed from the school. Religious congregations of all faiths gathered to pray for a peaceful end to the conflict and the NAACP fought the validity of the Sovereignty Commission and the forced registration of certain membership lists and organizations. One of those fined for not registering as a member of the NAACP was Daisy Bates, mentor to the nine students, who was fined $100

Photo on previous page: A collage shows the students known as the Little Rock Nine in 1957: (from top left) Gloria Ray, Terrence [sic] Roberts, Melba Pattillo [sic], Elizabeth Eckford, Ernest Green, Minnijean Brown, Jefferson Thomas, Carlotta Walls, and Thelma Mothershed. (© **MPI**/**Getty Images**.)

for not complying with the State Sovereignty Commission regulations.

Growing Violence

Throughout the school year, incidents of violence against the nine students grew. Verbal arguments and physical violence was common. The school received five bomb threats in a seven-day period in January 1958. That month, Minnijean Brown, one of the nine students, had chili dumped on her shoulders by a boy in the lunchroom. A month later, Brown called one of her tormenters "white trash" and was attacked by several bystanders. She said of the argument, "I just can't take everything they throw at me without fighting back. . . ." Brown was expelled—along with several other white students who had cards that read, "One down . . . eight to go" (these cards were distributed to the school students). After these incidents, Minnijean Brown left the school and moved to New York. The violence was not limited to the nine students—a white boy who talked with Ernest Green was verbally threatened and his car was vandalized.

The crisis at the school spilled over into the city of Little Rock. Segregationists threatened to boycott businesses that advertised in the *Arkansas Gazette* (which they viewed as being pro-integration). A new African-American organization, the Greater Little Rock Improvement League formed to end the crisis without pursuing litigation (counter to the actions of the NAACP). Meanwhile, the Capital Citizens Council and other segregationists continued to file legal action against integration of the city's schools. Local businessmen proposed alternate plans for desegregation which were supported by both the *Arkansas Gazette* and the *Arkansas Democrat*, but opposed by the NAACP, the Capital Citizens Coun-

> Throughout the school year, incidents of violence against the nine students grew.

cil, and the Mother's League (Governor Faubus remained non-committal), and Harry Ashmore, a journalist/editorialist for the *Arkansas Gazette*, received a Pulitzer Prize for his objectivity in covering the Little Rock Central High School Crisis.

By the time the first African-American student graduated from Little Rock Central High School in the spring of 1958, events had not calmed down. The only senior among the nine students, Ernest Green, was given his diploma while police and federal troops stood in attendance. Dr. Martin Luther King, Jr. attended the graduation ceremony virtually unnoticed. Green later commented, "It's been an interesting year. I've had a course in human relations first hand."

The US Supreme Court Bans Racial Segregation in Schools

Luther A. Huston

In the following viewpoint, legal and political writer Luther A. Huston reports in a 1954 newspaper article on the landmark US Supreme Court ruling that the segregation of children in public schools based on race is illegal because it denies children equal protection under the law. Lawyers for the states that segregated their students based on race argued that public education is a matter for the states to decide, not the federal government. The Supreme Court, however, sided with attorneys representing students from a variety of school districts in proclaiming that separate education is inherently unequal education.

Washington, May 17—The Supreme Court unanimously outlawed today racial segregation in public schools.

Chief Justice Earl Warren read two opinions that put the stamp of unconstitutionality on school systems in twenty-one states and the District of Columbia where segregation is permissive or mandatory.

'The doctrine of "separate but equal" has no place. Separate educational facilities are inherently unequal.'

The court, taking cognizance of the problems involved in the integration of the school systems concerned, put over until the next term, beginning October, the formulation of decrees to effectuate its 9-to-0 decision.

The opinions set aside the "separate but equal" doctrine laid down by the Supreme Court in 1896.

"In the field of public education," Chief Justice Warren said, "the doctrine of 'separate but equal' has no place. Separate educational facilities are inherently unequal."

He stated the question and supplied the answer as follows:

> We come then to the question presented: Does segregation of children in public schools solely on the basis of race, even though physical facilities and other "tangible" factors may be equal, deprive the children of the minority group of equal educational opportunities? We believe that it does.

States Stressed Rights

The court's opinion does not apply to private schools. It is directed entirely at public schools. It does not affect the "separate but equal doctrine" as applied on railroads and other public carriers entirely within states that have such restrictions.

The principal ruling of the court was in four cases involving state laws. The states' right to operate separated schools had been argued before the court on two occasions by representatives of South Carolina, Virginia, Kansas and Delaware.

In these cases, consolidated in one opinion, the high court held that school segregation deprived Negroes of "the equal protection of the laws guaranteed by the Fourteenth Amendment."

The other opinion involved the District of Columbia. Here schools have been segregated since Civil War days under laws passed by Congress.

"In view of our decision that the Constitution prohibits the states from maintaining racially segregated public schools," the Chief Justice said,

> It would be unthinkable that the same Constitution would impose a lesser duty on the Federal Government.
>
> We hold that racial segregation in the public schools of the District of Columbia is a denial of the due process of law guaranteeing by the Fifth Amendment to the Constitution.

The Fourteenth Amendment provides that no state shall "deny to any person within its jurisdiction the equal protection of the laws." The Fifth Amendment says that no person shall be "deprived of life, liberty or property without due process of law."

The seventeen states having mandatory segregation are Alabama, Arkansas, Delaware, Florida, Mississippi, Missouri, North Carolina, Oklahoma, Georgia, Kentucky, Louisiana, Maryland, South Carolina, Tennessee, Texas, Virginia and West Virginia.

Kansas, New Mexico, Arizona and Wyoming have permissive statutes, although Wyoming never has exercised it.

South Carolina and Georgia have announced plans to abolish public schools if segregation were banned.

Although the decision with regard to the constitutionality of school segregation was unequivocal, the

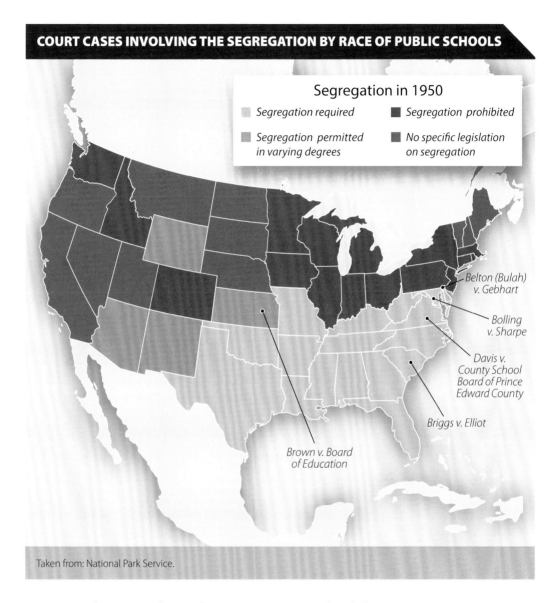

COURT CASES INVOLVING THE SEGREGATION BY RACE OF PUBLIC SCHOOLS

Segregation in 1950

Segregation required

Segregation permitted in varying degrees

Segregation prohibited

No specific legislation on segregation

Belton (Bulah) v. Gebhart

Bolling v. Sharpe

Davis v. County School Board of Prince Edward County

Briggs v. Elliot

Brown v. Board of Education

Taken from: National Park Service.

court set the cases down for reargument in the fall on questions that previously were argued last December. These deal with the power of the court to permit an effective gradual readjustment to school systems not based on color distinctions.

Other questions include whether the court itself should formulate detailed decrees and what issues should be dealt with. Also whether the cases should be remanded to the lower courts to frame decrees, and what general directions the Supreme Court should give the lesser tribunals if this were done.

Cases Argued Twice

The cases first came to the high court in 1952 on appeal from rulings of lower Federal courts, handed down in 1951 and 1952. Arguments were heard on Dec. 9–10, 1952.

Unable to reach a decision, the Supreme Court ordered rearguments in the present term and heard the cases for the second time on Dec. 7–8 last year.

Since then, each decision day has seen the courtroom packed with spectators awaiting the ruling. That was true today, though none except the justices themselves knew it was coming down. Reporters were told before the court convened that it "looked like a quiet day."

Three minor opinions had been announced, and those in the press room had begun to believe the prophesy when Banning E. Whittington, the court's press information officer, started putting on his coat.

"Reading of the segregation decisions is about to begin in the court room," he said. "You will get the opinions up there."

The courtroom is one floor up, reached by a long flight of marble steps. Mr. Whittington led a fast moving exodus. In the court room, Chief Justice Warren had just begun reading.

Each of the Associate Justices listened intently. They obviously were aware that no court since the *Dred Scott*[1] decision of March 6, 1857, had ruled on so vital an issue in the field of racial relations.

Dred Scott was a slave who sued for his freedom on the ground that he had lived in a territory where slavery was forbidden. The territory was the northern part of the Louisiana Purchase, from which slavery was excluded under the terms of the Missouri Compromise.

The Supreme Court ruled that Dred Scott was not a citizen who had a right to sue in the Federal courts, and that Congress had no constitutional power to pass the Missouri Compromise.

Thurgood Marshall, the lawyer who led the fight for racial equality in the public schools, predicted that there would be no disorder and no organized resistance to the Supreme Court's dictum.

He said that the people of the South, the region most heavily affected, were law-abiding and would not "resist the Supreme Court."

Association Calls Meetings

Mr. Marshall said that the state presidents of the National Association for the Advancement of Colored People would meet next week-end in Atlanta to discuss further procedures.

The Supreme Court adopted two of the major premises advanced by the Negroes in briefs and arguments presented in support of their cases.

Their main thesis was that segregation, of itself, was unconstitutional. The Fourteenth Amendment, which was adopted July 28, 1868, was intended to wipe out the last vestige of inequality between the races, the Negro side argued.

Against this, lawyers representing the states argued that since there was no specific constitutional prohibition against segregation in the schools, it was a matter for the states, under their police powers, to decide.

> Lawyers representing the states argued that . . . there was no specific constitutional prohibition against segregation [in] schools.

The Supreme Court rejected the "states' rights" doctrine, however, and found all laws ordering or permitting segregation in the schools to be in conflict with the Federal Constitution.

The Negroes also asserted that segregation had a psychological effect on pupils of the Negro race and was

The three lawyers who argued at the US Supreme Court on behalf of public school desegregation—(left to right) George E.C. Hayes, future Supreme Court justice Thurgood Marshall, and James M. Nabrit—pose for a celebratory photograph outside the court building the day the *Brown v. Board of Education* decision was announced. (© **AP Photo.**)

detrimental to the educational system as a whole. The court agreed.

"Today, education is perhaps the most important function of state and local governments," Chief Justice Warren wrote.

Compulsory school attendance laws and the great expenditures for education both demonstrate our recognition of the importance of education in our democratic society. It is the very foundation of good citizenship.

In these days it is doubtful that any child may reasonably be expected to succeed in life if he is denied the opportunity of an education. Such an opportunity, where the state has undertaken to provide it, must be made available to all on equal terms.

As to the psychological factor, the high court adopted the language of a Kansas court in which the lower bench held:

Segregation with the sanction of the law, therefore, has a tendency to retard the educational and mental development of Negro children and to deprive them of some of the benefits they would receive in a racially integrated school system.

1896 Doctrine Demolished

The "separate but equal" doctrine, demolished by the Supreme Court today, involved transportation, not education. It was the case of *Plessy vs. Ferguson*, decided in 1896. The court then held that segregation was not unconstitutional if equal facilities were provided for each race.

Since that ruling six cases have been before the Supreme Court, applying the doctrine to public education. In several cases, the court has ordered the admission to colleges and universities of Negro students on the ground that equal facilities were not available in segregated institutions.

Today, however, the court held the doctrine inapplicable under any circumstances to public education.

This means that the court may extend its ruling from primary and secondary schools to include state-supported colleges and universities. Two cases involving Negroes who wish to enter white colleges in Texas and Florida are pending before the court.

The question of "due process," also a clause in the Fourteenth Amendment, had been raised in connection with the state cases as well as the District of Columbia.

The High Court held, however, that since it had ruled in the state cases that segregation was unconstitutional under the "equal protection" clause, it was unnecessary to discuss "whether such segregation also violates the due process clause of the Fourteenth Amendment."

However, the "due process" clause of the Fifth Amendment was the core of the ruling in the District of Columbia case. "Equal protection" and "due process," the court noted, were not always interchangeable phrases.

'Segregation in public education . . . imposes on Negro children . . . a burden that constitutes an arbitrary deprivation of their liberty.'

Liberty Held Deprived

"Liberty under law extends to the full range of conduct which an individual is free to pursue, and it cannot be restricted except for a proper governmental objective," Chief Justice Warren asserted.

> Segregation in public education is not reasonably related to any proper governmental objective, and thus it imposes on Negro children of the District of Columbia a burden that constitutes an arbitrary deprivation of their liberty in violation of the due process clause.

Two principal surprises attended the announcement of the decision. One was its unanimity. There had been reports that the court was sharply divided and might not be able to get an agreement this term. Very few major rulings of the court have been unanimous.

The second was the appearance with his colleagues of Justice Robert H. Jackson. He suffered a mild heart attack on March 30. He left the hospital last week-end and had not been expected to return to the bench this term, which will end on June 7.

Perhaps to emphasize the unanimity of the court, perhaps from a desire to be present when the history-making verdict was announced, Justice Jackson was in his accustomed seat when the court convened.

Note

1. The *Dred Scott v. Sandford* (1857) US Supreme Court decision stated that people of African descent brought into the United States as slaves were not US citizens nor protected by the US Constitution. The landmark ruling applied to slaves and their descendants—slave or free.

The Governor of Arkansas Orders the State Militia to Block Black Students' Entry to Central High School

Orval E. Faubus

In the following viewpoint, Arkansas governor Orval E. Faubus addresses his constituents with a speech concerning his decision to call out the National Guard to prevent the integration of Central High School. He states that Arkansas has been and continues to be a "liberal and progressive" state and offers examples of the ways African Americans have been well treated in Arkansas. He then offers evidence that the people of Arkansas oppose integration of their schools. Finally he points to rumors and concerns about impending violence if Central High is integrated on September 3, 1957. For these reasons, Faubus has mobilized the National Guard and sent them to Little Rock.

SOURCE. Speech of Governor Orval Faubus, September 2, 1957. Orval Faubus Papers (MSF27/301) series 14, subseries 1, box 496. Special Collections, University of Arkansas Libraries, Fayetteville. Reproduced by permission.

Good evening, ladies and gentlemen of the television and radio audience.

In view of the decisions I have made, I think it is well to review for the people of the State and the nation, some of the background in the tense situation which has now developed relative to the forcible integration of the public schools of Little Rock.

Arkansas Is a Liberal and Progressive State

It is safe to say, to the informed and intelligent, that Arkansas has been known as a liberal and progressive State—perhaps the most liberal and progressive State in the South today. . . .

It is well known that Negroes are now in attendance and have been attending the University of Arkansas, a State institution, for a number of years.

Last year, members of the Negro race were enrolled in many State-supported colleges of Arkansas.

Also, Negroes have been integrated into the public school systems of the State, where it was acceptable to the majority and could be peaceably accomplished.

The public transportation systems of the State have been peaceably integrated, with no disorder and no untoward incidents except of a minor nature.

Negroes serve on both the Republican and Democratic State Central Committees, and Arkansas is the only State in the South where this is true.

A Negro elected by vote of the people serves on the Board of Aldermen of the City Government of Hot Springs.

Inclusion of African Americans in Arkansas

We also have in the State what is sometimes termed inter-racial sports events. For some years, professional football teams have played to capacity crowds in War

Memorial Stadium in Little Rock, with both teams having Negro members.

Last year in the Aluminum Bowl Game, the two outstanding small college teams of the nation competed in War Memorial Stadium. There were Negro members on both teams. It is well known that such competition is not permitted in some other States.

In the matter of the public school program, a part of the over-all progressive program adopted by the Legislature, teachers' salaries were increased an average of $810 annually in Arkansas. It is well known that the average increase for Negro teachers was in excess of the average increase for white teachers.

In the welfare program, the benefits have gone to the members of both races alike. On July 1st, of this year, the grants were increased $8.00 each per month. Also, a medical aid program has been set up for medically indigent people of the State.

African Americans Serve in State Government

Negroes have been given recognition, as is their due, in the field of State employment. They fill positions in the Education Department, in the Revenue Department, Highway Department, and other agencies of the State.

Negroes have been appointed by me and other Arkansas Governors to Boards and Commissions of the State. Many of these appointments required and received confirmation by the State Senate.

The Medical Center of Little Rock is not only an educational institution, but also a great charity and service facility. At the Center, a far greater proportion of the indigent people who receive treatment at State expense are members of the Negro race. . . .

During my time in office as Governor, I have never received any report of any effort to deprive the Negro citizen of his right to vote in any election throughout the seventy-five counties of the State. As the nation-wide audience and people of the State will recall, this was a subject of great controversy during the recent session of Congress in Washington, wherein much was said about civil rights measures to protect the Negro citizens' right to vote. I am proud now to say to you that no such action is necessary in the interest of the Negro, or any other minority, in Arkansas.

> "The citizens of Arkansas have been mindful of their problems as they relate to the good relations of the races.

These facts are given as irrefutable proof that the citizens of Arkansas have been mindful of their problems as they relate to the good relations of the races, that the citizenry as a whole have met their responsibilities in this and other fields, and that improvements and progress have been made in an orderly and peaceful manner.

The Forcible Integration of Little Rock Schools

We are now faced with a far different problem, and that is the forcible integration of the public schools of Little Rock against the overwhelming sentiment of the people of the area. This problem gives every evidence and indication that the attempt to integrate forcibly will bring about widespread disorder and violence.

There is another aspect which I must recognize, and that is the fact that this particular problem and its solution is not only State-wide, but nation-wide in scope. This, of course, is most unfortunate, but it is a situation *not* of my making.

The plan of integration now being forced upon us by the Federal Courts was set up by the Little Rock School Board and its Superintendent, and approved by a Federal Court prior to expressions of the people, which have been made manifest since that time. These expressions

Arkansas Governor Orval E. Faubus (1910–1994)

Orval E. Faubus served as the governor of Arkansas from 1955 through 1967. During these years, he became famous for his response to the US Supreme Court order that Little Rock public schools must be desegregated.

In September of 1957, Faubus faced a crisis: Nine African American students, now known as the Little Rock Nine, enrolled at the all-white Central High School in accordance with the 1954 *Brown v. Board of Education* decision that mandated integration and ended the long-standing practice of "separate but equal" facilities for African American citizens. Faubus governed many angry white people who were adamant that the African American students not be allowed to attend Central High.

Faubus chose to call up the Arkansas National Guard to prevent the Little Rock Nine from entering the school. This decision placed him at odds with US president Dwight D. Eisenhower, who federalized the Arkansas National Guard and sent them home. Eisenhower sent Army troops to Little Rock to assure the safety of the African American students.

Faubus's stand made him very popular with white voters, and he was returned to office four more times after the Little Rock crisis. At the same time, it is apparent that Faubus was never comfortable being associated with white supremacists; by all accounts, he was a moderate Democrat who reformed voting practices in Arkansas. Faubus left office in 1966, although he did attempt to retake the governorship in 1970, 1974, and 1986 without success.

Faubus's fortunes slid post–1966. Financially ruined, he had to sell his home and work as a bank teller. He and his wife divorced in 1969, his son committed suicide in 1976, and his second wife was murdered in 1983 while the couple was in the process of divorcing. Faubus died of cancer in 1994.

of the people have been clearly indicated by the greatest, time-honored principles of Democracy—by the exercise of the franchise at the ballot box, and the expressions of the members of the Legislature who are elected by and are the representatives of the people.

The Citizens of Arkansas Oppose Integration

Even the most extreme of these measures seeking to prevent the forcible integration of the schools against the people's will—the one known as the Johnson Amendment—was approved by the people by a vote of 185,374 to 146,064.

The Pupil Assignment measure seeks by constitutional and legal means to retain in the School Boards of the State some discretion and authority as to assignment of the pupils. It was approved by the people 214,713 to 121,129. The vote in Pulaski County, the area now most affected by the problem at hand, was 27,325 for, and 16,666 against.

The Resolution of Interposition, which sought to interpose the sovereignty of the State between the people (whom it is the duty of the State to protect) and any unjust and unwarranted interference of the Federal Government, was approved by a vote of 199,511 to 127,360. The vote on this measure in Pulaski County was 23,038 in favor, and 17,808 against.

It is a known fact that citizens who are not fully informed on ballot measures will usually vote against any amendment, rather than for it. If these numbers could be determined and subtracted from the opposition vote, the result would reveal that the people are even more overwhelmingly in favor of the measure than the actual vote indicates.

Furthermore, during the last session of the Legislature, four measures dealing with this and allied problems were passed overwhelmingly by both Houses. Only one vote was cast against any measure in the House, and in the Senate all the measures except one received two-thirds or more of the votes of the members of that body.

These measures, both those approved by vote of the people and those passed by the Legislature, are now upon the statute books of the State and to all intents and purposes are the law of the land at the present time. They will remain the law of the land until, by the proper authorities, they are declared to be otherwise.

Litigation seeking to determine the validity of these measures has now been filed in the Courts of the State and in the Federal Courts. There has not been sufficient time to adjudicate these measures to a final conclusion.

> "Imminence of disorder and violence . . . exists at this time in relation to the forcible integration of the schools."

Disorder and Unrest Is Imminent

To my mind, this is one of the greatest reasons for the unrest and for the imminence of disorder and violence which exists at this time in relation to the forcible integration of the schools tomorrow.

As the Governor of a sovereign State, pledged to uphold its laws and Constitution, to defend and protect the welfare of the people, and to preserve order and protect the rights of its citizens and their property, I feel strongly that time should be given to litigate these measures to final conclusion, in order that we may see clearly and unmistakably what is the law of the land—either State or Federal.

Now that a Federal Court has ruled no further litigation is possible before the forcible integration of Negroes and Whites in Central High School tomorrow, the evidence of discord, anger and resentment has come to me in a deluge from many, many sources. There is evidence of disorder and threats of disorder which could have but one inevitable result—that is, violence, which can lead to injury and harm to persons and property.

A police check has revealed a sale of unusually large numbers of weapons in the Little Rock area. The check reveals that some stores have completely sold out their

Arkansas governor Orval Faubus holds an August 1957 newspaper with front-page photos of violence in Little Rock caused by supporters for and against school integration. (© **AP Photo**.)

stocks of knives. These sales have been mostly to Negro youths, but many have been sold to Whites as well.

One store reported that a gang of Negro youths came as a group, and every one of its members purchased knives while another group waited outside. When the first group went out, the second group entered for the same purpose, whereupon the owner took his remaining stock of knives, locked it up, and declined to make further sales.

Last Thursday, I testified before the Chancery Court of Pulaski County in part as follows: "I have information that a number of revolvers were taken from students in high school, both White and Colored."

It is significant that Mr. House, Attorney for the School Board, did not cross-examine me on this statement. I can tell you why he declined—he knew the source of my information because the people he represented had the same information. They knew it was reliable, and that I had stated the truth.

In the same trial, Mr. Blossom, Superintendent of the Little Rock schools, testified he had been to see the Little Rock Chief of Police fifteen or twenty times to discuss the keeping of the peace at the opening of the school term. But Mr. Blossom declined to state that he anticipated violence. However, today, Mr. Blossom appealed to me for help.

The Fear of Violence Is Growing

I have undeniable reports of a telephone campaign of massive proportions going on in the City of Little Rock at this time, calling upon the mothers of White children to assemble peaceably upon the school grounds at 6:00 A.M. tomorrow, the opening day of school.

I have reports of caravans that will converge upon Little Rock from many points of the State, to assemble peaceably upon the school grounds in the morning. Some of these groups have already reached the city, and are here now. Some of the information about these caravans has come to me from the school authorities themselves.

Telephone calls have come to me at the mansion in a constant stream. The expressions of all are the fear of disorder and violence, and of the harm that may occur tomorrow in this attempt at forcible integration of Central High School.

Other evidence of the alarm and concern comes from a Negro newspaper.

Coming as a boy from the hills, from a family of modest circumstances, I learned and have treasured many of the time-honored adages.

"A stitch in time saves nine." "An ounce of prevention is worth a pound of cure."

Remembering the wisdom of these maxims, and being aware of the overwhelming evidence of impending disorder which could lead to violence and even bloodshed, I have therefore, in accordance with the solemn responsibilities and my Oath of Office, made the decision to act and to act now. It is only good judgment to act before the situation gets out of hand—before the resulting violence creates lasting enmity, animosity, and hate between citizens of this community, which would do irreparable harm to the good relations that have existed between the races. I have, therefore, taken the following action:

> Units of the National Guard have been, or are now being mobilized, with the mission to maintain or restore the peace and order of the community.

Units of the National Guard have been, or are now being mobilized, with the mission to maintain or restore the peace and order of the community. Advance units are already on duty on the grounds of Central High School.

The National Guard Has Been Mobilized

I have briefed the Commanders as to the situation, and they already have or are now briefing the members of their commands.

I have informed Chief Lindsey, Director of the Arkansas State Police, of the developments. He is now mobilizing a force to act as an arm of the State Militia in maintaining or restoring the peace and order of the community, and to act in every way possible to protect the lives and property of the citizens of Pulaski County.

This is a decision I have reached prayerfully. It has been made after conferences with dozens of people, and after checking and verifying as many of the reports as possible.

The mission of the State Militia is to maintain or restore order and to protect the lives and property of citizens. They will act not as segregationists or integrationists, but as soldiers called to active duty to carry out their assigned tasks.

I must state here, in all sincerity, it is my firm conviction that it will not be possible to restore or to maintain order and protect the lives and property of the citizens, if forcible integration is carried out tomorrow in the schools of this community. The inevitable conclusion, therefore, must be that the schools in Pulaski County, for the time being, must be operated on the same basis as they have been operated in the past.

I appeal now for reason, clear thinking, and good order. Let us all be good citizens, and continue as a people and as a State, upon the road of progress on which we have so enthusiastically embarked.

THE PUBLIC PEACE WILL BE PRESERVED!

President Eisenhower Addresses the Nation on the Situation in Little Rock

Dwight D. Eisenhower

In a speech to the American public, the US president describes the events in Little Rock, Arkansas, as African American students are denied entry to Central High School. Eisenhower views this as an obstruction to federal law and announces that he has ordered federal troops to Little Rock to uphold the US Supreme Court order to desegregate the school. He insists that national laws are supreme and that the rights of the Little Rock Nine will be upheld.

Good Evening, My Fellow Citizens:
For a few minutes this evening I want to speak to you about the serious situation that has arisen

SOURCE. Dwight D. Eisenhower, "Radio and Television Address to the American People on the Situation in Little Rock," September 24, 1957. Dwight D. Eisenhower Memorial Commission.

in Little Rock. To make this talk I have come to the President's office in the White House. I could have spoken from Rhode Island, where I have been staying recently, but I felt that, in speaking from the house of Lincoln, of Jackson and of Wilson, my words would better convey both the sadness I feel in the action I was compelled today to take and the firmness with which I intend to pursue this course until the orders of the Federal Court at Little Rock can be executed without unlawful interference.

Mobs Are Obstructing Justice in Little Rock

In that city, under the leadership of demagogic extremists, disorderly mobs have deliberately prevented the carrying out of proper orders from a Federal Court. Local authorities have not eliminated that violent opposition and, under the law, I yesterday issued a Proclamation calling upon the mob to disperse.

This morning the mob again gathered in front of the Central High School of Little Rock, obviously for the purpose of again preventing the carrying out of the Court's order relating to the admission of Negro children to that school.

> I have today issued an Executive Order directing the use of troops under Federal authority to aid in the execution of Federal law at Little Rock, Arkansas.

Whenever normal agencies prove inadequate to the task and it becomes necessary for the Executive Branch of the Federal Government to use its powers and authority to uphold Federal Courts, the President's responsibility is inescapable.

In accordance with that responsibility, I have today issued an Executive Order directing the use of troops under Federal authority to aid in the execution of Federal law at Little Rock, Arkansas. This became necessary when my Proclamation of yesterday was not observed, and the obstruction of justice still continues.

It is important that the reasons for my action be understood by all our citizens.

Ordering Federal Troops to Little Rock

As you know, the Supreme Court of the United States has decided that separate public educational facilities for the races are inherently unequal and therefore compulsory school segregation laws are unconstitutional.

Our personal opinions about the decision have no bearing on the matter of enforcement; the responsibility and authority of the Supreme Court to interpret the Constitution are very clear. Local Federal Courts were instructed by the Supreme Court to issue such orders and decrees as might be necessary to achieve admission to public schools without regard to race—and with all deliberate speed.

US president Dwight D. Eisenhower deployed the 101st Airborne Division to Central High School in Little Rock on September 24, 1957, to enforce the adoption of federal integration laws and protect the African American students at the school. (© A.Y. Owen/ Time & Life Pictures/ Getty Images.)

During the past several years, many communities in our Southern States have instituted public school plans for gradual progress in the enrollment and attendance of school children of all races in order to bring themselves into compliance with the law of the land.

They thus demonstrated to the world that we are a nation in which laws, not men, are supreme.

I regret to say that this truth—the cornerstone of our liberties was not observed in this instance.

It was my hope that this localized situation would be brought under control by city and State authorities. If the use of local police powers had been sufficient, our traditional method of leaving the problems in those hands would have been pursued. But when large gatherings of obstructionists made it impossible for the decrees of the Court to be carried out, both the law and the national interest demanded that the President take action.

Here is the sequence of events in the development of the Little Rock school case.

The Sequence of Events

In May of 1955, the Little Rock School Board approved a moderate plan for the gradual desegregation of the public schools in that city. It provided that a start toward integration would be made at the present term in the high school, and that the plan would be in full operation by 1963. Here I might say that in a number of communities in Arkansas integration in the schools has already started and without violence of any kind. Now this Little Rock plan was challenged in the courts by some who believed that the period of time as proposed in the plan was too long.

The United States Court at Little Rock, which has supervisory responsibility under the law for the plan of desegregation in the public schools, dismissed the challenge, thus approving a gradual rather than an abrupt change from the existing system. The court found that the school board had acted in good faith in planning for a public school system free from racial discrimination.

Since that time, the court has on three separate occasions issued orders directing that the plan be carried out. All persons were instructed to refrain from interfering with the efforts of the school board to comply with the law.

Proper and sensible observance of the law then demanded the respectful obedience which the nation has a right to expect from all its people. This, unfortunately, has not been the case at Little Rock. Certain misguided persons, many of them imported into Little Rock by agitators, have insisted upon defying the law and have sought to bring it into disrepute. The orders of the court have thus been frustrated.

> "Certain misguided persons . . . have insisted upon defying the law and have sought to bring it into disrepute."

The very basis of our individual rights and freedoms rests upon the certainty that the President and the Executive Branch of Government will support and insure the carrying out of the decisions of the Federal Courts, even, when necessary with all the means at the President's command.

Unless the President did so, anarchy would result. There would be no security for any except that which each one of us could provide for himself.

The interest of the nation in the proper fulfillment of the law's requirements cannot yield to opposition and demonstrations by some few persons.

Mob rule cannot be allowed to override the decisions of our courts.

Federal Troops Will Prevent Interference with Court Orders

Now, let me make it very clear that Federal troops are not being used to relieve local and state authorities of

Presidential Proclamation 3204: Obstruction of Justice in the State of Arkansas

WHEREAS, certain persons in the State of Arkansas, individually and in unlawful assemblages, combinations, and conspiracies have willfully obstructed the enforcement of orders of the United States District Court for the Eastern District of Arkansas with respect to matters relating to enrollment and attendance at public schools, particularly at Central High School, located in Little Rock School District, Little Rock, Arkansas; and

WHEREAS, such willful obstruction of justice hinders the execution of the laws of that State and of the United States, and makes it impracticable to enforce such laws by the ordinary course of judicial proceedings; and

WHEREAS, such obstruction of justice constitutes a denial of the equal protection of the laws secured by the Constitution of the United Sates and impedes the course of justice under those laws;

NOW, THEREFORE, I, Dwight D. Eisenhower, President of the United States, under and by virtue of the authority vested in me by the Constitution and the Statutes of the United States, including Chapter 15 of Title 10 of the United States Code, particularly Sections 332, 333 and 334 thereof, do command all persons engaged in such obstruction of justice to cease and desist therefrom, and to disperse forthwith.

IN WITNESS THEREOF, I have hereunto set my hand and caused the Seal of the United States of America to be affixed.

DONE at the City of Newport, Rhode Island this twenty-third day of September in the year of our Lord nineteen hundred and fifty-seven, and of the Independence of the United States of America the one hundred and eighty-second.

DWIGHT D. EISENHOWER

SOURCE. Dwight D. Eisenhower, "Proclamation 3204, September 23, 1957." www.eisenhower.archives.gov.

their primary duty to preserve the peace and order of the community. Nor are the troops there for the purpose of taking over the responsibility of the School Board and the other responsible local officials in running Central

High School. The running of our school system and the maintenance of peace and order in each of our States are strictly local affairs and the Federal Government does not interfere except in a very few special cases and when requested by one of the several States. In the present case the troops are there, pursuant to law, solely for the purpose of preventing interference with the orders of the Court.

The proper use of the powers of the Executive Branch to enforce the orders of a Federal Court is limited to extraordinary and compelling circumstances. Manifestly, such an extreme situation has been created in Little Rock. This challenge must be met and with such measures as will preserve to the people as a whole their lawfully-protected rights in a climate permitting their free and fair exercise.

The overwhelming majority of our people in every section of the country are united in their respect for observance of the law even in those cases where they may disagree with that law.

They deplore the call of extremists to violence.

The decision of the Supreme Court concerning school integration, of course, affects the South more seriously than it does other sections of the country. In that region I have many warm friends, some of them in the city of Little Rock. I have deemed it a great personal privilege to spend in our Southland tours of duty while in the military service and enjoyable recreational periods since that time.

So from intimate personal knowledge, I know that the over whelming majority of the people in the South—including those of Arkansas and of Little Rock—are of good will, united in their efforts to preserve and respect the law even when they disagree with it.

They do not sympathize with mob rule. They, like the rest of our nation, have proved in two great wars their readiness to sacrifice for America.

The Foundation of the American Way

A foundation of our American way of life is our national respect for law.

In the South, as elsewhere, citizens are keenly aware of the tremendous disservice that has been done to the people of Arkansas in the eyes of the nation, and that has been done to the nation in the eyes of the world.

At a time when we face grave situations abroad because of the hatred that Communism bears toward a system of government based on human rights, it would be difficult to exaggerate the harm that is being done to the prestige and influence, and indeed to the safety, of our nation and the world.

Our enemies are gloating over this incident and using it everywhere to misrepresent our whole nation. We are portrayed as a violator of those standards of conduct which the peoples of the world united to proclaim in the Charter of the United Nations. There they affirmed "faith in fundamental human rights" and "in the dignity and worth of the human person" and they did so "without distinction as to race, sex, language or religion."

> I call upon the citizens of the State of Arkansas to assist in bringing to an immediate end all interference with the law and its processes.

And so, with deep confidence, I call upon the citizens of the State of Arkansas to assist in bringing to an immediate end all interference with the law and its processes. If resistance to the Federal Court orders ceases at once, the further presence of Federal troops will be unnecessary and the City of Little Rock will return to its normal habits of peace and order and a blot upon the fair name and high honor of our nation in the world will be removed.

Thus will be restored the image of America and of all its parts as one nation, indivisible, with liberty and justice for all.

Good night, and thank you very much.

Arkansas Prohibits Racial Integration in Public Schools

Arkansas General Assembly

In the following viewpoint, the General Assembly of the State of Arkansas claims that most people in Arkansas oppose integration of public schools as well as the use of federal troops to enforce integration. As a consequence, the assembly passes a law during an extraordinary session providing for separate educational facilities for white and African American children. Furthermore the law states that students can refuse to attend classes with students of another race. Finally the assembly declares that the law is necessary to keep the peace.

AN ACT to Provide Separate Classes for Instruction in the Public Schools of Arkansas for Children of the White and Negro Races Under

---

SOURCE. "Acts of the Sixty-Second General Assembly of the State of Arkansas, August 26, 1958," University of Arkansas Libraries, August 26, 1958. Special Collections, University of Arkansas Libraries, Fayetteville. Reproduced by permission.

Closing the Public Schools in Little Rock

Those who would integrate our schools at any price are still among us. They have seized upon the present situation to promote and foment concern and discontent, because of the temporary closing of the schools. They have spread wild rumors and attempted to organize demonstrations. These are the same people and the same forces who have all along been opposed to the majority will of the people of Little Rock and Arkansas. . . .

It was with a heavy heart that I found it necessary to sign the bills of the Extraordinary Session of the General Assembly and to close the High Schools in the City of Little Rock. I took this action only after the last hope of relief from an intolerable situation had been exhausted.

The Supreme Court shut its eyes to all the facts, and in essence said— integration at any price, even if it means the destruction of our school system, our educational processes, and the risk of disorder and violence that could result in the loss of life— perhaps yours. . . .

Certain Conditions, to Provide a Choice of Classes for Students Under Certain Conditions, to Provide Penalties for Interference With a Student's Choice of Classes, and for Other Purposes.

WHEREAS, the Supreme Court of the United States predicated its school integration decision upon the psychological effect of segregated classes upon children of the Negro race, and, at the same time, ignored the psychological impact of integrated schools upon certain white children who observe segregation of the races as a way of life; and

WHEREAS, legislation is necessary in order to protect the health, welfare, well-being, and educational opportunities for such white children;

NOW, THEREFORE,

Be It Enacted by the General Assembly of the State of Arkansas:

Our own educational people have testified that a suitable educational system at Little Rock cannot be maintained on an integrated basis. Why, then, should we even attempt to keep these schools open as public schools when, based upon this sworn testimony, they clearly do not meet our constitutional provisions for a suitable and efficient system of education? We have a perfect right to close these schools as public institutions, and once closed and found to be not needed for public purposes, the school board has the right and the authority under a law that has been on our statute books for 83 years, to lease these buildings and facilities to a bona fide private agency [that is, convert them to private, segregated schools].

SOURCE. *"Excerpts from the Speech of Governor Orval E. Faubus, September 18, 1958," Orval Eugene Faubus Papers, Special Collections, University of Arkansas. http://libinfo.uark.edu.*

SECTION 1. No student shall ever be denied the right to enroll in, and receive instruction in, any course in any public school in the State of Arkansas by reason of his or her refusal to attend a class with a student of another or different race.

SECTION 2. Any person who interferes or attempts to interfere through coercion, intimidation, or otherwise, with a student's choice of classes, as set forth in Section 1 hereof, shall be guilty of a misdemeanor and, upon conviction, shall be punished by a fine of not less than one hundred dollars ($100.00) and not more than five hundred dollars ($500.00); and, in addition to such fine, such person shall be confined to the county jail for a period of not less than thirty (30) days and not more than ninety (90) days, and shall be ineligible for public office or employment by the State of Arkansas or any political sub-division thereof for a period of three years.

In September 1958, Arkansas high school students show their support for Governor Orval Faubus. To derail local efforts to integrate public education, the governor and the State General Assembly closed all public schools for the 1958–1959 school year. (© Francis Miller/ **Time & Life Pictures/ Getty Images.**)

SECTION 3. It has been found and it is hereby declared by the General Assembly that a large majority of the people of this State are opposed to the forcible integration of, or mixing of the races in, the public schools of the State; that practically all of the people of this State are opposed to the use of federal troops in aid of such integration; that the people of this State are opposed to the use of any federal power to enforce the integration of the races in the public schools; that it is now threatened that Negro children will be forcibly enrolled and permitted to attend some of the public schools of this State formerly attended only by white children; that the President of the United States has indicated that federal troops may be used to enforce the orders of the District Court respecting enrollment and attendance of Negro pupils in schools formerly attended only by white school children; that the forcible operation of a public school in this State attended by both Negro and white children will inevitably result in violence in and about the school and throughout the district involved endangering safety of buildings and other property and lives; that the state of feeling of the great majority of the people of this State is such that the forcible mixing of the races in public schools will seriously impair the operation of a suitable and efficient system of schools, and result in lack of discipline in the schools; that for said reasons it is hereby declared necessary for the public peace, health and safety that this Act shall become effective without delay. An emergency, therefore, exists and this Act shall take effect and be in force from and after its passage.

> The forcible mixing of the races in public schools will seriously impair the operation of a suitable and efficient system of schools.

The US Supreme Court Rules the Arkansas Law Unconstitutional

Supreme Court of the United States

In the following viewpoint, the Supreme Court of the United States rules that an Arkansas law passed in an emergency session to circumvent the court's order to integrate the state's schools is unconstitutional. The justices opine that the actions of the Arkansas governor and legislature prevented the Little Rock Nine students from attending school until federal troops intervened. The justices reiterate that students may not be barred from attending classes because of their race, as well as firmly reasserting that states do not have the right to circumvent federal law.

U nder a plan of gradual desegregation of the races in the public schools of Little Rock, Arkansas, adopted by petitioners and approved by the courts below, respondents, Negro children, were ordered

---

SOURCE. Supreme Court of the United States, *Cooper v. Aaron*, 358 US 1 (1958), September 12, 1958.

admitted to a previously all-white high school at the beginning of the 1957–1958 school year. Due to actions by the Legislature and Governor of the State opposing desegregation, and to threats of mob violence resulting therefrom, respondents were unable to attend the school until troops were sent and maintained there by the Federal Government for their protection; but they attended the school for the remainder of that school year. Finding that these events had resulted in tensions, bedlam, chaos and turmoil in the school, which disrupted the educational process, the District Court, in June 1958, granted petitioners' request that operation of their plan of desegregation be suspended for two and one-half years, and that respondents be sent back to segregated schools. The Court of Appeals reversed. Held: The judgment of the Court of Appeals is affirmed, and the orders of the District Court enforcing petitioners' plan of desegregation are reinstated, effective immediately.

Examining the Case

1. This Court cannot countenance a claim by the Governor and Legislature of a State that there is no duty on state officials to obey federal court orders resting on this Court's considered interpretation of the United States Constitution in *Brown v. Board of Education* [1954].

2. This Court rejects the contention that it should uphold a suspension of the Little Rock School Board's plan to do away with segregated public schools in Little Rock until state laws and efforts to upset and nullify its holding in the *Brown* case have been further challenged and tested in the courts.

3. In many locations, obedience to the duty of desegregation will require the immediate general admission of Negro children, otherwise qualified as students for their appropriate classes, at particular schools.

4. If, after analysis of the relevant factors (which, of course, excludes hostility to racial desegregation),

a District Court concludes that justification exists for not requiring the present nonsegregated admission of all qualified Negro children to public schools, it should scrutinize the program of the school authorities to make sure that they have developed arrangements pointed toward the earliest practicable completion of desegregation, and have taken appropriate steps to put their program into effective operation.

5. The petitioners stand in this litigation as the agents of the State, and they cannot assert their good faith as an excuse for delay in implementing the respondents' constitutional rights, when vindication of those rights has been rendered difficult or impossible by the actions of other state officials.

6. The constitutional rights of respondents are not to be sacrificed or yielded to the violence and disorder which have followed upon the actions of the Governor and Legislature, and law and order are not here to be preserved by depriving the Negro children of their constitutional rights.

7. The constitutional rights of children not to be discriminated against in school admission on grounds of race or color declared by this Court in the *Brown* case can neither be nullified openly and directly by state legislators or state executives or judicial officers, nor nullified indirectly by them through evasive schemes for segregation whether attempted "ingeniously or ingenuously."

8. The interpretation of the Fourteenth Amendment enunciated by this Court in the *Brown* case is the supreme law of the land, and Art. VI of the Constitution makes it of binding effect on the States "any Thing in the Constitution or Laws of any State to the Contrary notwithstanding."

9. No state legislator or executive or judicial officer can war against the Constitution without violating his solemn oath to support it. . . .

10. State support of segregated schools through any arrangement, management, funds or property cannot be squared with the command of the Fourteenth Amendment that no State shall deny to any person within its jurisdiction the equal protection of the laws. . . .

The Majority Decision

As this case reaches us it raises questions of the highest importance to the maintenance of our federal system of government. It necessarily involves a claim by the Governor and Legislature of a State that there is no duty on state officials to obey federal court orders resting on this Court's considered interpretation of the United States Constitution. Specifically it involves actions by the Governor and Legislature of Arkansas upon the premise that they are not bound by our holding in *Brown v. Board of Education*. That holding was that the Fourteenth Amendment forbids States to use their governmental powers to bar children on racial grounds from attending schools where there is state participation through any arrangement, management, funds or property. We are urged to uphold a suspension of the Little Rock School Board's plan to do away with segregated public schools in Little Rock until state laws and efforts to upset and nullify our holding in *Brown v. Board of Education* have been further challenged and tested in the courts. We reject these contentions. . . .

The following are the facts and circumstances so far as necessary to show how the legal questions are presented.

On May 17, 1954, this Court decided that enforced racial segregation in the public schools of a State is a denial of the equal protection of the laws enjoined by the Fourteenth Amendment. The Court postponed,

> [Cooper v. Aaron] raises questions of the highest importance to the maintenance of our federal system of government.

Members of the Little Rock school board (left to right) Virgil Blossom, Wayne Upton, and Dale Alford, enter the US Supreme Court in August 1958 as plaintiffs in *Cooper v. Aaron*. The Supreme Court ruled against the board in the case but found that the board acted in good faith to desegregate schools. (© **Ed Clark/ Time & Life Pictures/ Getty Images.**)

pending further argument, formulation of a decree to effectuate this decision. That decree was rendered May 31, 1955. In the formulation of that decree the Court recognized that good faith compliance with the principles declared in Brown might in some situations "call for elimination of a variety of obstacles in making the transition to school systems operated in accordance with the constitutional principles set forth in our May 17, 1954, decision.". . .

Under such circumstances, the District Courts were directed to require "a prompt and reasonable start toward full compliance," and to take such action as was necessary to bring about the end of racial segregation in the public schools "with all deliberate speed." Of course, in many locations, obedience to the duty of desegregation would require the immediate general admission of Negro children, otherwise qualified as students for their appropriate classes, at particular schools. On the other hand, a District Court, after analysis of the relevant factors (which, of course, excludes hostility to racial desegregation), might conclude that justification existed for not requiring the present nonsegregated admission of all qualified Negro children. In such circumstances, however, the courts should scrutinize the program of the school authorities to make sure that they had developed arrangements pointed toward the earliest practicable completion of desegregation, and had taken appropriate steps to put their program into effective operation. It was made plain that delay in any guise in order to deny the constitutional rights of Negro children could not be countenanced, and that only a prompt start, diligently and earnestly pursued, to eliminate racial segregation from the public schools could constitute good faith compliance. State authorities were thus duty bound to devote every effort toward initiating desegregation and bringing about the elimination of racial discrimination in the public school system.

Preparing a Plan for Public School Desegregation in Little Rock

On May 20, 1954, three days after the first *Brown* opinion, the Little Rock District School Board adopted, and on May 23, 1954, made public, a statement of policy entitled "Supreme Court Decision—Segregation in Public Schools." In this statement the Board recognized that

> It is our responsibility to comply with Federal Constitutional Requirements and we intend to do so when the Supreme Court of the United States outlines the method to be followed.

Thereafter the Board undertook studies of the administrative problems confronting the transition to a desegregated public school system at Little Rock. It instructed the Superintendent of Schools to prepare a plan for desegregation, and approved such a plan on May 24, 1955, seven days before the second *Brown* opinion. The plan provided for desegregation at the senior high school level (grades 10 through 12) as the first stage. Desegregation at the junior high and elementary levels was to follow. It was contemplated that desegregation at the high school level would commence in the fall of 1957, and the expectation was that complete desegregation of the school system would be accomplished by 1963. Following the adoption of this plan, the Superintendent of Schools discussed it with a large number of citizen groups in the city. As a result of these discussions, the Board reached the conclusion that "a large majority of the residents" of Little Rock were of "the belief . . . that the Plan, although objectionable in principle," from the point of view of those supporting segregated schools, "was still the best for the interests of all pupils in the District."

Upon challenge by a group of Negro plaintiffs desiring more rapid completion of the desegregation process, the District Court upheld the School Board's plan. . . .

While the School Board was thus going forward with its preparation for desegregating the Little Rock school system, other state authorities, in contrast, were actively pursuing a program designed to perpetuate in Arkansas the system of racial segregation which this Court had held violated the Fourteenth Amendment. First came, in November 1956, an amendment to the State Constitution flatly commanding the Arkansas General Assembly to oppose "in every Constitutional manner the Un-constitutional desegregation decisions of May 17, 1954 and May 31, 1955 of the United States Supreme Court," Ark. Const., Amend. 44, and, through

> Other state authorities, in contrast [to the Little Rock school board], were actively pursuing a program designed to perpetuate . . . racial segregation.

the initiative, a pupil assignment law, Ark. Stat. 80-1519 to 80-1524. Pursuant to this state constitutional command, a law relieving school children from compulsory attendance at racially mixed schools, Ark. Stat. 80-1525, and a law establishing a State Sovereignty Commission, Ark. Stat. 6-801 to 6-824, were enacted by the General Assembly in February 1957.

The School Board and the Superintendent of Schools nevertheless continued with preparations to carry out the first stage of the desegregation program. Nine Negro children were scheduled for admission in September 1957 to Central High School, which has more than two thousand students. Various administrative measures, designed to assure the smooth transition of this first stage of desegregation, were undertaken.

The Arkansas Governor Takes Action

On September 2, 1957, the day before these Negro students were to enter Central High, the school authorities were met with drastic opposing action on the part of the Governor of Arkansas who dispatched units of the Arkansas National Guard to the Central High School grounds and placed the school "off limits" to colored students. As found by the District Court in subsequent proceedings, the Governor's action had not been requested by the school authorities, and was entirely unheralded. . . .

The Governor's action caused the School Board to request the Negro students on September 2 not to attend the high school "until the legal dilemma was solved." The next day, September 3, 1957, the Board petitioned the District Court for instructions, and the court, after a hearing, found that the Board's request of the Negro students to stay away from the high school had been made because of the stationing of the military guards by the state authorities. The court determined that this was not a reason for departing from the approved plan, and ordered the School Board and Superintendent to proceed with it.

On the morning of the next day, September 4, 1957, the Negro children attempted to enter the high school but, as the District Court later found, units of the Arkansas National Guard "acting pursuant to the Governor's order, stood shoulder to shoulder at the school grounds and thereby forcibly prevented the 9 Negro students . . . from entering," as they continued to do every school day during the following three weeks.

That same day, September 4, 1957, the United States Attorney for the Eastern District of Arkansas was requested by the District Court to begin an immediate investigation in order to fix responsibility for the interference with the orderly implementation of the District Court's direction to carry out the desegregation program. Three days later, September 7, the District Court denied a petition of the School Board and the Superintendent of Schools for an order temporarily suspending continuance of the program. . . .

The National Guard was then withdrawn from the school.

The next school day was Monday, September 23, 1957. The Negro children entered the high school that morning under the protection of the Little Rock Police Department and members of the Arkansas State Police. But the officers caused the children to be removed from the school during the morning because they had difficulty controlling a large and demonstrating crowd which had gathered at the high school. . . . On September 25, however, the President of the United States dispatched federal troops to Central High School and admission of the Negro students to the school was thereby effected. Regular army troops continued at the high school until November 27, 1957. They were then replaced by federalized National Guardsmen who remained throughout the balance of the school year. Eight of the Negro students remained in attendance at the school throughout the school year.

Examining the Present Case

We come now to the aspect of the proceedings presently before us. On February 20, 1958, the School Board and the Superintendent of Schools filed a petition in the District Court seeking a postponement of their program for desegregation. Their position in essence was that because of extreme public hostility, which they stated had been engendered largely by the official attitudes and actions of the Governor and the Legislature, the maintenance of a sound educational program at Central High School, with the Negro students in attendance, would be impossible. The Board therefore proposed that the Negro students already admitted to the school be withdrawn and sent to segregated schools, and that all further steps to carry out the Board's desegregation program be postponed for a period later suggested by the Board to be two and one-half years. . . .

In affirming the judgment of the Court of Appeals which reversed the District Court we have accepted without reservation the position of the School Board, the Superintendent of Schools, and their counsel that they displayed entire good faith in the conduct of these proceedings and in dealing with the unfortunate and distressing sequence of events which has been outlined. We likewise have accepted the findings of the District Court as to the conditions at Central High School during the 1957–1958 school year, and also the findings that the educational progress of all the students, white and colored, of that school has suffered and will continue to suffer if the conditions which prevailed last year are permitted to continue.

The significance of these findings, however, is to be considered in light of the fact, indisputably revealed by the record before us, that the conditions they depict are directly traceable to the actions of legislators and executive officials of the State of Arkansas, taken in their official capacities, which reflect their own determination to resist this Court's decision in the *Brown* case and which have brought about violent resistance to that decision in Arkansas. . . .

> "The constitutional rights of [African American students] are not to be sacrificed or yielded to . . . the actions of the [Arkansas] Governor and Legislature."

The constitutional rights of respondents are not to be sacrificed or yielded to the violence and disorder which have followed upon the actions of the Governor and Legislature. As this Court said some 41 years ago in a unanimous opinion in a case involving another aspect of racial segregation: "It is urged that this proposed segregation will promote the public peace by preventing race conflicts. Desirable as this is, and important as is the preservation of the public peace, this aim cannot be accomplished by laws or ordinances which deny rights created or protected by the Federal Constitution." Thus law and order are not here to be preserved by depriving the Negro children of their constitutional rights. The record before us clearly establishes that the growth of the Board's difficulties to a magnitude beyond its unaided power to control is the product of state action. Those difficulties, as counsel for the Board forthrightly conceded on the oral argument in this Court, can also be brought under control by state action.

The controlling legal principles are plain. The command of the Fourteenth Amendment is that no "State" shall deny to any person within its jurisdiction the equal protection of the laws. "A State acts by its legislative, its executive, or its judicial authorities. It can act in no other way. The constitutional provision, therefore, must mean that no agency of the State, or of the officers or agents by whom its powers are exerted, shall deny to any person within its jurisdiction the equal protection of the laws. . . ." In short, the constitutional rights of children not to be discriminated against in school admission on grounds of race or color declared by this Court in the *Brown* case can neither be nullified openly and directly by state legislators or state executive or judicial officers, nor nullified indirectly by them through evasive schemes for segregation whether attempted "ingeniously or ingenuously."

What has been said, in the light of the facts developed, is enough to dispose of the case. However, we should answer the premise of the actions of the Governor and Legislature that they are not bound by our holding in the *Brown* case. It is necessary only to recall some basic constitutional propositions which are settled doctrine.

No state legislator or executive or judicial officer can war against the Constitution without violating his undertaking to support it. Chief Justice Marshall spoke for a unanimous Court in saying that: "If the legislatures of the several states may, at will, annul the judgments of the courts of the United States, and destroy the rights acquired under those judgments, the constitution itself becomes a solemn mockery. . . ." A Governor who asserts a power to nullify a federal court order is similarly restrained. If he had such power, said Chief Justice Hughes, in 1932, also for a unanimous Court, "it is manifest that the fiat of a state Governor, and not the Constitution of the United States, would be the supreme law of the land; that the restrictions of the Federal Constitution upon the exercise of state power would be but impotent phrases.". . .

It is, of course, quite true that the responsibility for public education is primarily the concern of the States, but it is equally true that such responsibilities, like all other state activity, must be exercised consistently with federal constitutional requirements as they apply to state action. The Constitution created a government dedicated to equal justice under law. The Fourteenth Amendment embodied and emphasized that ideal. State support of segregated schools through any arrangement, management, funds, or property cannot be squared with the Amendment's command that no State shall deny to any person within its jurisdiction the equal protection of the laws. The right of a student not to be segregated on racial grounds in schools so maintained is indeed so fundamental and pervasive that it is embraced in the concept of due process of law. The basic decision in *Brown* was unanimously reached by this Court only after the case had been briefed and twice argued and the issues had been given the most serious consideration. Since the first *Brown* opinion three new Justices have come to the Court. They are at one with the Justices still on the Court who participated in that basic decision as to its correctness, and that decision is now unanimously reaffirmed. The principles announced in that decision and the obedience of the States to them, according to the command of the Constitution, are indispensable for the protection of the freedoms guaranteed by our fundamental charter for all of us. Our constitutional ideal of equal justice under law is thus made a living truth.

CHAPTER 2

Controversies Surrounding the Little Rock Nine Crisis

President Eisenhower Acted Wisely by Sending Federal Troops to Little Rock

The Nation

In the following viewpoint, the editors of *The Nation* magazine argue that President Dwight D. Eisenhower acted responsibly in sending federal troops to Little Rock, Arkansas, to uphold the ruling of the US Supreme Court that schools should be integrated. The writers assert that while there may be minor violence in enforcing the ruling, it is incumbent upon the federal government to ensure that individual citizens are able to exercise their constitutional rights; in this case, students who want to study at an integrated high school. The writers conclude that the integration of public schools should not be considered tragic in any way.

SOURCE. "This Is No Tragedy," *The Nation*, vol. 185, no. 10, October 5, 1957, pp. 205–206. Copyright © 1957 by The Nation. Reprinted with permission from the October 5, 1957, issue of The Nation. For subscription information, call 1-800-333-8536. Portion of each week's The Nation magazine can be accessed at www.thenation.com.

The President [Dwight D. Eisenhower] has acted firmly, wisely, and in fulfillment of his constitutional responsibilities in ordering federal troops into Little Rock to uphold the authority of the federal courts. Sooner or later the President would have had to face this direct challenge, if not in Arkansas then elsewhere. For the country now knows, if it did not know before, that a large section of the South has long been nurtured on the misconception that compliance with the Thirteenth, Fourteenth, and Fifteenth Amendments is a matter of local option. (The Jackson *Daily News*, in an editorial of September 25, comments: "To the President—Nuts!"). The President met the Little Rock crisis in the only way he could meet it; he said what needed to be said and did what needed to be done.

The President Has Precedent

Over a year ago (July 7, 1956), in a special issue [of *The Nation*] on the theme, "Time to Kill Jim Crow," we said in these columns that there was ample precedent for the use of federal troops and that the President should use them, if necessary, to secure compliance with decrees issued pursuant to the Supreme Court's ruling. In the same editorial, we pointed out that the repeated assurances, official and otherwise, that federal troops would not be used had the effect of encouraging Southern officials to resist the inevitable. In retrospect, it is amazing that so many responsible leaders should have acquiesced in the proposition that force should never be used under any circumstances whatever to obtain compliance with federal district court desegregation decrees. Even the President—and he was supported by Adlai Stevenson—encouraged the South to believe that force would not be used. But *any* President, Republican or Democrat, must use force, if necessary, to uphold the Constitution. The President should have made it clear, throughout the period subsequent to May 17, 1954, that he would use

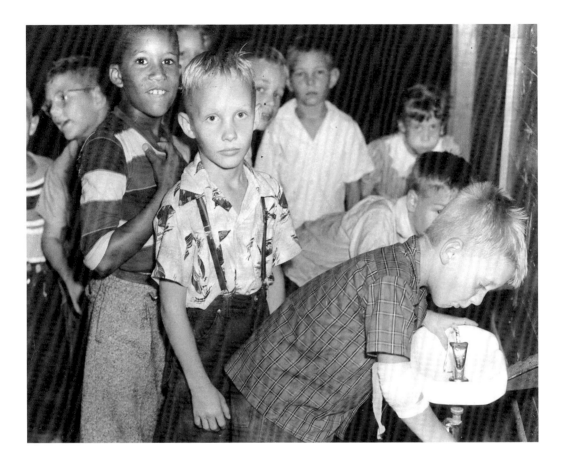

Children at an integrated elementary school in North Carolina use the water fountain on October 3, 1951. Desegregation was a fact of life in some states even before the landmark *Brown v. Board of Education* decision. (© **AP Photo.**)

whatever force was necessary to secure compliance. But whatever the President's sins of omission, the Senators who signed the Dixiecrat Manifesto[1] were more grievously at fault; they encouraged a form of insurrection. What has been needed all along has been strong executive and legislative leadership in support of the Supreme Court's ruling. Now that the President has acted, a new climate of opinion will form which should make it possible to proceed "with all deliberate speed" to enforce desegregation as a national policy.

Of course there will be "incidents" and "disturbances"; hoodlums will howl and hysterics will rant. Teen-age girls will scream, "Oh, God, they let the n------ in!" Ignorant mobs will shout, "two, four, six, eight, we ain't gonna integrate." Photographers will have their cameras smashed. Senator Byrd's blood pressure will continue to rise. Talmadge II will rumble imprecations throughout Georgia. Klansmen will light fiery crosses in the dead of night. Spinsters will faint. And, here and there, troops may be needed, for short periods of time, to maintain order—but only in those communities where local "law and order" has connived at violence. The conservative South will not rush headlong into open rebellion; already these elements are preparing the way for a reluctant but gradual capitulation. Racial demagogues always use the threat of "bloodshed" and "violence" to intimidate the majority of law-abiding citizens who, of course, abhor physical violence of any kind. But it is folly ever to yield to such threats. If the liberty of an individual is to be suppressed because the granting of that liberty may incite others to violence, then the effect is to make the least educated and most intemperate citizens the arbiters of what shall or shall not be permitted. The precondition to the solution of the so-called "race problem" in the South has always been the equal enforcement of the law and of every right sanctioned by the Constitution.

Integration Is Not a Tragedy

As amazing as the blindness to this obvious truth has been, even more amazing is the somber tragic note which echoes in most of the editorial and other comments on Little Rock. "Tragedy in the Sunshine," writes [columnist] Stewart Alsop; "a national disaster," intones [presidential candidate] Adlai Stevenson; "The Tragedy of Little Rock," sighs the *Wall Street Journal*. One learns from a story in the *New York Post* that the career of Virgil T. Blossom, Little Rock's Superintendent of Schools, has been "wrecked" by "the great, great tragedy" that has taken place. (Our impression, from this distance, is that Mr. Blossom's career has not been blighted but that,

overnight, he has acquired an enviable national reputation.) In some of this comment, the Supreme Court
is accused of having "changed" the
settled law of the land—query: when
was the Fourteenth Amendment re-
pealed?—and of having "legislated" a
policy of desegregation. "The tragedy
begins," comments the *Wall Street
Journal*, "with nine men who decided
to remake the country"—that is, a
unanimous court reversed a decision
that nine out of ten law school deans
would now agree misinterpreted and largely nullified the
historic purpose of the Fourteenth Amendment.

> "In what sense and in whose eyes is the use of federal troops in Little Rock a matter of tragic national concern?

Then in what sense and in whose eyes is the use of
federal troops in Little Rock a matter of tragic national
concern? In a sense, of course, it is tragic when some
of the citizens of a democracy exhibit an incapacity for
self-government. No one likes to see American citizens,
however few in number, held back, at the point of bayonets, from assaulting Negro children. And admittedly
there is cause for some concern over the consequence
that may arise once the troops are withdrawn. But we
have managed to escape the tragedy that would have
ensued if the President had not acted as he did; in fact,
we narrowly averted a disaster, in terms of world opinion. Little Rock is surely no tragedy for the gallant Mrs.
L.C. Bates who heads the NAACP [National Association
for the Advancement of Colored People] in Arkansas,
nor for the Negro children now enrolled and attending
Central High. In fact, there is no cause for any of us to
weep, as though a vast tragedy had engulfed the nation,
over those front-page photographs of the Negro children
walking up the *front* steps of Central High flanked by
federal troops. The real tragedy, if tragedy we must find,
is that Negroes were not admitted there long ago, without troops.

No Tears for Jim Crow

The "battle" of Little Rock is over. Casualties: three minor injuries, one accidental. The appearance of federal troops and bayonets, the *New York Times* correspondent notes, did not have an inflammatory effect; it had a sobering effect. In a city of 117,000 (20,000 of them Negroes), agitators could not draw more than 1,500 whites to the school area. "The vast majority of Little Rock citizens went about their normal business. Downtown was quiet." So brush aside those crocodile tears; let's weep no more for Jim Crow.[2]

Notes

1. An effort by Southern senators to stop integration.
2. Jim Crow laws were those that required segregation of the races.

President Eisenhower Did Not Have the Authority to Send Federal Troops to Little Rock

R. Carter Pittman

In the following viewpoint, R. Carter Pittman argues that any powers not granted specifically to the federal government by the US Constitution are retained by the state. He further argues that President Eisenhower did not act in accordance with the Constitution when he elected to send federal troops to Little Rock, Arkansas, to enforce integration of Central High. Moreover, he asserts that the US Supreme Court acted unconstitutionally in its rulings concerning integration and that the court does not have the power to enact law. Pittman was an attorney from Dalton, Georgia, and an expert on the US Constitution.

SOURCE. R. Carter Pittman, "The Federal Invasion of Arkansas in Light of the Constitution," *American Mercury*, February 1958, pp. 117–122. Reprinted with permission of Mr. R. Carter Pittman Jr.

S ince the Federal Government is a parchment Government created by a written instrument, which we know as the Constitution, all officers of that Government, including the President, must look to that parchment for every power that they exercise, whether in Washington or in Little Rock. That is true, not only of the President; but of the Congress and of the Federal Courts.

States Retain Rights Not Granted to the Federal Government

If a power is not granted to federal officers by the Constitution itself such power is retained by the States or by the people.

The Tenth Amendment states that truism, but that was true before the Tenth Amendment was adopted. It was spelled out merely to settle and satisfy the minds of those who were fearful of the evils that lurked in the shadows of the new and untried government. Thus, the Federal Constitution is the power-of-attorney of those whose offices were created by the Constitution.

The exercise of a power not granted in the Constitution itself is usurpation. The usurpation of power creates no legal authority. Upon the integrity of that principle rests the validity of every right man has ever wrested from power and every liberty he has ever torn from tyrants. The soundness of that proposition is not disputed among men of learning and honor anywhere.

So, we must search the Constitution to see if we can find authority for the actions of President Eisenhower in sending federal troops to Little Rock and in federalizing Arkansas troops. There are only two provisions of the Constitution relating to such a situation.

One, relating to the use of federalized state troops, appears in Article I and the other, relating to the use of federal troops, appears in Article IV of the Constitution. The latter provides that the United States shall protect each state "against invasion; and on Application of the

Legislature, or of the Executive (when the Legislature *cannot* be convened) against domestic violence."

The State of Arkansas Did Not Request Assistance

Obviously, there has been no invasion or threatened invasion of Arkansas, hence the President had no authority to send federal troops into Arkansas, except upon the application of the Legislature of Arkansas for the purpose of putting down domestic violence. The Legislature of Arkansas did not ask for federal troops and since there is no reason why it could not be convened, the Governor of Arkansas has no authority to call on the President to send federal troops. If the Governor of Arkansas had such authority he has not exercised it. Therefore, the President had no authority to send federal troops into Arkansas under any fair construction of Section 4 of Article IV or of any other provision of the Constitution.

The other provision relating to the use of military force by the President, in Section 8 of Article I, empowers the Congress "to provide for calling forth the Militia to execute the Laws of the Union, suppress Insurrection and repel Invasion."

> Obviously, there has been no invasion or threatened invasion of Arkansas, hence the President had no authority to send federal troops.

Obviously, there was no insurrection to be suppressed and no invasion to be repelled in Arkansas; therefore, the Congress had no power to authorize the President to call forth, or federalize the state troops or militia of Arkansas, unless it was "to execute the laws of the Union."

Shortly after the Civil War and during the reconstruction period the Congress, while led by sadistic men, attempted to authorize the President to federalize state troops under certain conditions. It is not necessary to examine those acts because the authority of the Congress

itself is limited by the specific constitutional provision quoted.

The Supreme Court Does Not Make Laws

The final and crucial question is whether or not the President acted "to execute the Laws of the Union" in accordance with the Constitution. The answer to that question answers all questions as to the existence of an "insurrection."

What are the "Laws of the Union"? The phrase "the Laws of the Union" has the identical meaning as the phrase "the law of the land," which is defined in Article

A federal soldier points his rifle as protesters gather in the streets during the Little Rock Nine crisis of 1957. Some legal scholars argue that the situation at the school did not meet any of the requirements for federal military action in a state. (© **Hulton Archive/Getty Images.**)

VI as "this Constitution, and the laws of the United States which shall be made in pursuance thereof"; (and treaties). *A decision of the Supreme Court of the United States or any other federal court is excluded by the definition itself.* As a matter of fact, Article III of the Constitution provides that the judicial power of federal court may not extend to any *case* arising under federal "law," unless that law be "this Constitution, the Laws of the United States, and treaties made, or which shall be made, under their authority," thus repeating the definition of "the law of the land."

The Courts Derive Power from the Constitution

No federal or state court of record in America has ever held that a decision of the Supreme Court of the United States or that of any other federal court is "the law of the land" or "the Law of the Union." Such decision is never anything more than *the law of the case* actually decided by the court and binding only upon the parties to that case and on no others. As was said by Charles Warren, in his *History of the Supreme Court,* page 748, Volume 2:

> However the court may interpret the provisions of the Constitution, it is still the Constitution which is the law and not the decision of the court.

Federal courts must look to the Constitution for their powers and their jurisdiction the same as the President and the Congress. If jurisdiction is not conferred by the Constitution it cannot be conferred by the Supreme Court itself. Only the Congress may make a federal law under authority granted in the very first line of the Constitution, which vests the power to make law in the Congress. The First Amendment predicates our most precious Freedom on the proposition that only the Congress may make a federal law.

The common law is not a part of the body of federal laws as it is a part of the body of state laws. Hence all federal laws must be "made" by lawmakers in the manner provided in the Constitution. When *made* they are written to be read, while state laws may be unwritten. A decision of the Supreme Court of a state expounding or declaratory of common law may, in a sense, become *a law of the state* until changed by the legislature of that state, when that state has adopted or inherited the common law, as have all American states except Louisiana. The federal courts are bound by the common law of the states, in diversity of citizenship cases, as declared by the highest courts of the states. The Federal Constitution did not adopt the common law; hence federal courts must hunt the law within the four corners of the Constitution or within the bounds of statutes or treaties. If federal courts find "the law of the land" or "the Law of the Union" elsewhere they must go to sociology or to alien philosophy—and their judges become usurpers. If there is "insurrection" in Arkansas it is against the laws of Arkansas—not against any federal laws.

It is contended by some that the 14th Amendment is involved and that such Amendment constitutes a "law of the Union" authorizing the use of state troops by the President. If we concede that the 14th Amendment was legally adopted it provides how it is to be implemented and enforced. That was not left to chance, caprice—or to Warren. It says in its last clause that only the Congress has the power to implement or enforce it. If one line of the Amendment is legal, the last line is legal. If that Amendment confers power on the Congress to legislate with respect to segregated schools (which need not be discussed here), the Congress has passed no law since its adoption relating to segregated schools in Arkansas or in any other State, except to establish segregated schools in the District of Columbia and to sanction them in laws relating to the distribution of surplus commodities in the schools of the states.

The Supreme Court Decision Was Sociological Not Legal

"The law of the land" and "the law of the Union" is the same today as it was on May 16, 1954, as it was in 1927 when a unanimous Supreme Court bench upheld segregated schools in *Gong Lum vs. Rice,* as was held in *Plessy vs. Ferguson* in 1896, with one judge dissenting, and as it was during all preceding and intervening years. The Supreme Court rested its integration decision of May 17, 1954, on sociological writings—not on the Constitution. An alien socialist, [Karl Gunnar] Myrdal, of socialistic Sweden, was substituted by Warren and Frankfurter for Mason, Franklin, Morris, Wilson, Madison and Marshall.

> When the Militia of Arkansas was federalized . . . the State of Arkansas lost constitutional freedom and its people lost security from despotism.

There is no "law of the Union" on which the President's order may legally rest. Since the President had no "law of the Union" to enforce in Little Rock he had no Constitutional authority to federalize Arkansas troops.

The second paragraph of the Bill of Rights records a lot of forgotten history. It says: "A well regulated Militia, being necessary to the security of a *free* State, the right of the people to keep and bear Arms, shall not be infringed."

When the Militia of Arkansas was federalized by President Eisenhower's edict, the State of Arkansas lost constitutional freedom and its people lost security from despotism.

What is said here relates to *right*—not *might.*

It relates to Constitutional power—not usurped power. Boss Tweed once said, "the way to have power is to take it." President Eisenhower has torn a page out of that notorious old man's philosophical book; he has not used a page or a paragraph from *any* law book.

Public School Segregation Is Unconstitutional

Supreme Court of the United States

In the following viewpoint, the US Supreme Court, in the 1954 landmark case *Brown v. Board of Education of Topeka*, overturns the policy of "separate but equal" educational facilities and declares segregation by race in public schools to be unconstitutional. The court bases its decision on the Fourteenth Amendment of the US Constitution, the amendment that guarantees all citizens equal protection under the law. The court opines that segregation harms the development of African American children and must be abolished. The ruling sets the stage for the enrollment of the Little Rock Nine at Central High School.

Segregation of white and Negro children in the public schools of a State solely on the basis of race, pursuant to state laws permitting or requiring

SOURCE. Supreme Court of the United States, *Brown v. Board of Education*, 347 US 483 (1954), May 17, 1954.

such segregation, denies to Negro children the equal protection of the laws guaranteed by the Fourteenth Amendment—even though the physical facilities and other "tangible" factors of white and Negro schools may be equal.

(a) The history of the Fourteenth Amendment is inconclusive as to its intended effect on public education.

(b) The question presented in these cases must be determined not on the basis of conditions existing when the Fourteenth Amendment was adopted, but in the light of the full development of public education and its present place in American life throughout the Nation.

(c) Where a State has undertaken to provide an opportunity for an education in its public schools, such an opportunity is a right which must be made available to all on equal terms.

(d) Segregation of children in public schools solely on the basis of race deprives children of the minority group of equal educational opportunities, even though the physical facilities and other "tangible" factors may be equal.

(e) The "separate but equal" doctrine adopted in *Plessy v. Ferguson, 163 U.S. 537* [1896], has no place in the field of public education.

(f) The cases are restored to the docket for further argument on specified questions relating to the forms of the decrees.

> Segregation of children in public schools solely on the basis of race deprives children of the minority group of equal educational opportunities.

Chief Justice Earl Warren's Opinion

These cases come to us from the States of Kansas, South Carolina, Virginia, and Delaware. They are premised on different facts and different local conditions, but a common legal question justifies their consideration together in this consolidated opinion.

Dismantling the Separate but Equal Doctrine

In a limited sense the *Brown v. Topeka Board of Education* (1954) decision overturned the "separate but (un)equal" doctrine. It dealt with de jure segregation in public schools, in which governmental agents (school boards) required blacks and whites to attend different schools. The Court ruled this an unconstitutional violation of blacks' Fourteenth Amendment rights because it "has a detrimental effect upon the colored children" in that it suggests an inferiority among blacks that weakens their motivation to learn and negatively affects their hearts and minds, thereby depriving them of equal educational opportunity. Because of delaying tactics by many state and local officials, little racial integration occurred in schools for ten years. In truth, the *Brown* decision was the tip of the iceberg that punctured the "separate but (un)equal" doctrine.

It was based on prior precedent-setting lawsuits by the National Association for the Advancement of Colored People (NAACP) that challenged racial segregation and on the dissemination of psychological and sociological research on the negative effects of racial segregation. Finally, and perhaps most importantly, victory against segregation beyond the schools was the product of social activism and pressure created by public protests, boycotts, and disruptions of the status quo (including the Montgomery bus boycott, sit-ins, and riots after the assassination of Dr. Martin Luther King Jr.) that forced many authorities to see that they had more to lose than to gain in preserving state-sanctioned racial segregation.

SOURCE. *"Separate-but-Equal,"* International Encyclopedia of the Social Sciences, *ed. William A. Darity Jr., vol. 7. Detroit: Macmillan Reference USA, 2008, pp. 445–447.

In each of the cases, minors of the Negro race, through their legal representatives, seek the aid of the courts in obtaining admission to the public schools of their community on a nonsegregated basis. In each instance, they had been denied admission to schools attended by white children under laws requiring or permitting segregation according to race. This segregation was alleged to deprive the plaintiffs of the equal protection of the laws under the Fourteenth Amendment. In each of the cases other than the Delaware case, a three-judge federal district court denied relief to the plaintiffs on the so-called "separate but equal" doctrine announced by this Court in *Plessy v. Ferguson, 163 U.S. 537.* Under that doctrine, equality of treatment is accorded when the races are provided substantially equal facilities, even though these facilities [are] separate. In the Delaware case, the Supreme Court of Delaware adhered to that doctrine, but ordered that the plaintiffs be admitted to the white schools because of their superiority to the Negro schools.

The plaintiffs contend that segregated public schools are not "equal" and cannot be made "equal," and that hence they are deprived of the equal protection of the laws. Because of the obvious importance of the question presented, the Court took jurisdiction. Argument was heard in the 1952 Term, and reargument was heard this Term on certain questions propounded by the Court.

The Historical Background of Segregated Schools

Reargument was largely devoted to the circumstances surrounding the adoption of the Fourteenth Amendment in 1868. It covered exhaustively consideration of the Amendment in Congress, ratification by the states, then-existing practices in racial segregation, and the views of proponents and opponents of the Amendment. This discussion and our own investigation convince us that, although these sources cast some light, it is not enough to resolve the problem with which we are faced. At best, they are inconclusive. The most avid proponents of the post–War Amendments undoubtedly intended them to remove all legal distinctions among "all persons born or naturalized in the United States." Their opponents, just as certainly, were antagonistic to both the letter and the spirit of the Amendments and wished them to have the most limited effect. What others in Congress and the state legislatures had in mind cannot be determined with any degree of certainty.

An additional reason for the inconclusive nature of the Amendment's history with respect to segregated schools is the status of public education at that time. In the South, the movement toward free common schools, supported by general taxation, had not yet taken hold. Education of white children was largely in the hands of private groups. Education of Negroes was almost nonexistent, and practically all of the race [was] illiterate. In fact, any education of Negroes was forbidden by law in some states. Today, in contrast, many Negroes have achieved outstanding success in the arts and sciences, as well as in the business and professional world. It is true that public school education at the time of the Amendment had advanced further in the North, but the effect of the Amendment on Northern States was generally ignored in the congressional debates. Even in the North, the conditions of public education did not approximate those existing today. The curriculum was usually rudimentary; ungraded schools were common in rural areas; the school term was but three months a year in many states, and compulsory school attendance was virtually unknown. As a consequence, it is not surprising that there should be so little in the history of the Fourteenth Amendment relating to its intended effect on public education. . . .

In approaching this problem, we cannot turn the clock back to 1868, when the Amendment was adopted, or even to 1896, when *Plessy v. Ferguson* was written. We must consider public education in the light of its full development and its present place in American life throughout the Nation. Only in this way can it be determined if segregation in public schools deprives these plaintiffs of the equal protection of the laws.

A classroom in a segregated black grade school in 1956 shows the substandard conditions that the US Supreme Court argued violated the Equal Protection Clause of the Constitution. (© **Gordon Parks/Time & Life Pictures/Getty Images.**)

Segregation Generates Inequality

Today, education is perhaps the most important function of state and local governments. Compulsory school attendance laws and the great expenditures for education both demonstrate our recognition of the importance of education to our democratic society. It is required in the performance of our most basic public responsibilities, even service in the armed forces. It is the very foundation of good citizenship. Today it is a principal instrument in awakening the child to cultural values, in preparing him for later professional training, and in helping him to adjust normally to his environment. In these days, it is doubtful that any child may reasonably be expected to succeed in life if he is denied the opportunity of an education. Such an opportunity, where the state has undertaken to provide it, is a right which must be made available to all on equal terms.

> It is doubtful that any child may reasonably be expected to succeed in life if he is denied the opportunity of an education.

We come then to the question presented: Does segregation of children in public schools solely on the basis of race, even though the physical facilities and other "tangible" factors may be equal, deprive the children of the minority group of equal educational opportunities? We believe that it does. . . .

Segregation of white and colored children in public schools has a detrimental effect upon the colored children. The impact is greater when it has the sanction of the law, for the policy of separating the races is usually interpreted as denoting the inferiority of the negro group. A sense of inferiority affects the motivation of a child to learn. Segregation with the sanction of law, therefore, has a tendency to [retard] the educational and mental development of negro children and to deprive them of some of the benefits they would receive in a racial[ly] integrated school system.

Whatever may have been the extent of psychological knowledge at the time of *Plessy v. Ferguson*, this finding is amply supported by modern authority. Any language in *Plessy v. Ferguson* contrary to this finding is rejected.

We conclude that, in the field of public education, the doctrine of "separate but equal" has no place. Separate educational facilities are inherently unequal. Therefore, we hold that the plaintiffs and others similarly situated for whom the actions have been brought are, by reason of the segregation complained of, deprived of the equal protection of the laws guaranteed by the Fourteenth Amendment. This disposition makes unnecessary any discussion whether such segregation also violates the Due Process Clause of the Fourteenth Amendment.

Integration Is Not a Valid Part of the US Constitution

David Lawrence

In the following viewpoint, David Lawrence, a columnist for *US News & World Report*, argues that the Fourteenth Amendment of the US Constitution was not ratified in a lawful way, making it an invalid part of the Constitution. As a consequence, any rulings of the US Supreme Court based on the Fourteenth Amendment are also invalid. He further argues that there is nothing in the Constitution that gives the judiciary branch of government the right to control or regulate schools. Finally he asserts that the Constitution does not grant the president the right to use National Guard troops to enforce Supreme Court rulings.

President [Dwight D.] Eisenhower, in telegraphing to the Governor of Arkansas last week, said:

SOURCE. David Lawrence, "Which 'Constitution'?," *US News & World Report*, vol. 43, September 13, 1957, p. 128. Copyright © 1957 by US News & World Report. All rights reserved. Reproduced by permission.

When I became President, I took an oath to support and defend the Constitution of the United States. The only assurance I can give you is that the Federal Constitution will be upheld by me by every legal means at my command.

But which Constitution?

Is the so-called Fourteenth Amendment, under which "integration" is being forced today upon an unwilling population in the South, really a valid part of the Constitution?

Is the Fourteenth Amendment Valid?

The Southern States, after the war was over, ratified the Thirteenth Amendment abolishing slavery and this was accepted as legal by the Federal Government. Yet when the same legislatures in the South subsequently assembled lawfully and rejected in due form a proposed Fourteenth Amendment, all Southern members of Congress were deprived of their seats in the Senate and the House. Federal troops were ordered to take charge of these State legislatures. Puppet legislatures finally did "ratify" under duress.

The Supreme Court in the last 89 years has never ventured in a single instance to decide the issue of whether this "ratification" was actually lawful.

Why, therefore, are some of us so explicit and eloquent nowadays in sanctifying the phrase—the "supreme law of the land"—as requiring compliance with the vague and undefined edicts of a Supreme Court that has plainly disregarded the illegality of the so-called Fourteenth Amendment?

> Where in the Constitution are the federal courts given the right to control or regulate the schools of the nation?

Where in the Constitution are the federal courts given the right to control or regulate the schools of the nation and to dictate to them whom they shall admit as students and whom they shall refuse to admit?

Where in the Constitution is there any delegation of power to the Federal Government to put in jail parents who wish to persuade other parents to refrain from sending their children to mixed schools? Yet federal injunctions today seek to coerce these citizens and deprive them of their right to speak freely as guaranteed under the First Amendment of the Constitution.

States' Rights vs. the Federal Government

The President's telegram to the Governor of Arkansas will become a historic document. It may have unfortunate consequences in the future relations between the States and the Federal Government. It appears to be an ill-advised statement prepared for Mr. Eisenhower by

A crowd protests against desegregation in Arkansas in 1959, the year the US Supreme Court reviewed a new law enacting segregation in the state. Critics strongly believed that it was unconstitutional for the federal government to require racial integration. (© Buyenlarge/Getty Images.)

The US Constitution's Equal Protection Clause

Equal protection as a legal concept is the idea that individuals should be treated in the same manner as other individuals in similar circumstances. The Equal Protection Clause of the Fourteenth Amendment to the U.S. Constitution provides that "no state shall . . . deny to any person within its jurisdiction the equal protection of the laws." According to the U.S. Supreme Court, the Due Process Clause of the Fifth Amendment also has an "equal protection component," protecting against arbitrary or unreasonable discrimination by the federal government.

Adopted during the five years following the Civil War, the Thirteenth, Fourteenth, and Fifteenth Amendments abolished slavery, extended U.S. citizenship to slaves and descendants of former slaves, ensured the right to vote regardless of race, and gave Congress the power to enforce these guarantees through legislation. In that context, the Fourteenth Amendment's Equal Protection Clause was intended to provide equal rights for blacks, and that was the view taken by the U.S. Supreme Court in the first case in which the clause was invoked. According to the Court in the *Slaughterhouse Cases* (1873), the purpose of the Equal Protection Clause was to protect "Negroes as a class" from discrimination "on account of their race."

In subsequent decisions, however, the U.S. Supreme Court limited both the scope and the substance of the Constitution's equal protection guarantee. In the *Civil Rights Cases* (1883), the Court ruled that Congress's authority to enforce the Fourteenth Amendment applied only to government actors, not private individuals. Thus, Congress could not use its enforcement power to prohibit racial discrimination in places such as hotels, restaurants, and theaters. And in *Plessy v. Ferguson* (1897), the Court held that state laws requiring "equal but separate" facilities for blacks and whites did not violate the Equal Protection Clause, because the Fourteenth Amendment guaranteed political equality but not social equality. According to the *Plessy* Court, denying blacks the right to serve on juries deprived them of equal protection of the laws, but maintaining dual school systems for black and white students did not. With these decisions, the Supreme Court gave constitutional sanction to racial segregation in education, transportation, public accommodations, employment, and housing.

SOURCE. *Malia Reddick, "Equal Protection,"* International Encyclopedia of the Social Sciences, *ed. William A. Darity Jr., second edition, vol. 2. Detroit: Macmillan Reference USA, 2008, pp. 614–616.*

overzealous lawyers in the Department of Justice. The telegram said in part:

> You and other State officials—as well as the National Guard, which is, of course, uniformed, armed and partially sustained by the Federal Government—will, I am sure, give full cooperation to the United States District Court.

Where in the Constitution is any power given to the President or to anyone in the Federal Government to say to the Governor of a sovereign State that he must not use the National Guard—State troops—to maintain order? And since when does the fact that the National Guard receives funds or uniforms or guns from the Federal Government deprive the Governors of our States of their right to use these troops for State purposes without first obtaining the permission of the Federal Government?

Does this mean, too, that the allocation of federal funds to schools, which has been urgently advocated in recent months by the President, will give the Federal Government some new and hitherto unbestowed grant of power to pass judgment on the efficiency of a State Governor or to question his motives when he attempts to do his duty, as he sees it, under the Constitution of his own State as well as the Constitution of the United States?

Since when, to be sure, is it the duty of the National Guard to execute federal injunctions? Since when has the National Guard become an instrument of the federal judiciary? Since when has an injunction or order issued by a lower court become a final decree that must be obeyed under threats of reprisals by the Chief Executive even before the court order has been properly reviewed on appeal to the higher courts?

Are the Governors and State legislatures now mere puppets, and have our several States suddenly become "satellites" which can function only with the consent of a federal dictatorship?

Federal Judges Should Not Usurp Power

There is only one Federal Constitution in America. It is in the Articles and lawfully-adopted Amendments to the document itself. All misguided attempts to amend this Constitution by the fiat of nine judges must be deplored as a usurpation of power and a defiance of the Constitution itself.

For to the people alone—uncoerced by military force—is given the power to change the Constitution. The method is specifically prescribed in the Constitution itself.

This is the way to preserve our dual system of government. It is the only way by which the nation can maintain internal peace and national unity.

The Little Rock Nine Students and Families Suffered Harm and Danger for the Sake of Justice

Christine Firer Hinze

In the following viewpoint, theologian Christine Firer Hinze argues that the Little Rock Nine's families were right to allow their children to participate in the struggle for public school integration. Hinze refutes an earlier essay by political theorist Hannah Arendt, who argued that racial integration should be addressed in the political arena instead of schools and that forced integration violates parents' rights. Hinze, however, says that while parents must protect

SOURCE. Christine Firer Hinze, "Reconsidering Little Rock: Hannah Arendt, Martin Luther King Jr., and Catholic Social Thoughts on Children and Families in the Struggle for Justice," *Journal of the Society of Christian Ethics*, vol. 29, no. 1, 2009, pp. 25–50. Copyright © 2009 by Society of Christian Ethics. All rights reserved. Reproduced by permission.

children from harm, they must also teach children about hope and justice. In her view, the families involved in the crisis should be commended for their exemplary courage in the face of danger.

The disagreement between [political philosopher] Hannah Arendt and black leaders over the ethics of involving children in civil rights action had much to do with the way theoretical claims about justice depend upon, and intersect with, embodied particularities experienced within and around families. Arendt's political theory was impelled by a passionate commitment to the concrete. Both her political philosophy and her life experience, especially empathy for the plight of the "unwelcome child," underlay her support for the rights of minorities but also her doubts concerning the effectiveness of a campaign for racial justice that focused on enforced integration of the public schools. . . .

For Arendt, court-ordered school desegregation in Little Rock was problematic for three reasons: it targeted the wrong battle; it took place in the wrong context, the schools; and it used the wrong combatants, children. . . .

[Arendt's essay] "Reflections on Little Rock" drew harsh responses from both white and black critics. Although he never issued a formal rebuttal to Arendt's essay, Martin Luther King Jr. contended that the struggle for civil rights was as much for and about children as it was adults and that to strategically engage families and children in the struggle for civil rights was both legitimate and salutary. King's speeches, his public and family life, and the movement as a whole embody eloquent responses to the objections raised by Arendt and bespeak alternative ways of addressing her concerns about children in the public realm. In their circumstances, the witness of King and family participants in the civil rights movement counterindicate Arendt's effort to rigidly separate the social and political spheres, her judgments concerning children's vulnerability and adults' responsibility, and her understanding (or lack thereof) of the worth and meaning of familial risk and sacrifice for the sake of public ends.

Racism Affects the Personal, the Social, and the Political

At the historical moment in which the Little Rock Nine gained notoriety and Hannah Arendt wrote her "Reflections," African Americans in the United States were experiencing critical momentum in a struggle against institutional racism that had been ongoing since the end of the Civil War. As [author] Cornel West puts it, black justice-seekers during this period focused their principal attentions on "the racist institutional structures in the United States which rendered the vast majority of black people politically powerless (deprived of the right to vote or participate in governmental affairs), economically exploited (in dependent positions as sharecroppers or in unskilled jobs), and socially degraded (separate, segregated, and unequal eating and recreational facilities, housing, education, transportation, and police protection)." The movement that Martin Luther King Jr. came to symbolize recognized racism's mutually reinforcing entrenchment in each of these areas—the political, the economic, and the social—and thus sought, through a variety of nonviolent but assertive strategies, to combat it on all three fronts.

By arguing that racial exclusion ought to be resisted only on the "political" front, Arendt failed to take into account the fact that institutional racism—of which southern Jim Crow segregation was but one egregious example—was sustained not only by laws but also by force of powerful ideology and habituated social custom backed by violence and terror. Lynchings and Ku Klux Klan activities did not need to be frequent to maintain a climate that deterred the majority of the black population, fearing for their families' safety, from openly resisting their subordinate and exploited social, economic, and political status.

Arendt's critique, ironically for one whose political philosophy demanded attention to concrete particulars and to historical specificity, neither examined nor took fully into account the particularities of southern black families' situation. For them, the personal-familial, social-economic, and legal-political effects of racism were profoundly intertwined. Nor did she grasp the significance of a historical moment when legal and judicial support for dismantling racist institutions seemed newly

Ellis Thomas (left) supports and advises his son, Jefferson—one of the Little Rock Nine—at their home in September 1958. (© Bettmann/ Corbis.)

within reach. Hope that real change was at last possible energized African American families who chose to engage in what was, on Arendt's own terms, genuinely political action. By marching, registering voters, rallying, or participating in school integration programs, families publicly acted in concert, in ways intended to bring forth and shore up something new in the common world. Far from self-interested "social climbing," this political action entailed danger and sacrifice, but its anticipated fruits, which included the recovery of participants' agency and self-respect in public, were deemed worth the risks.

We can get a better sense of how the embodied particularities of southern black families' situations warranted their decisions to involve children in the fight for racial justice by further considering how experiences of children's vulnerability and family responsibility, interacting with a potent spiritual perspective on suffering and the cross, yielded aspects of the Little Rock situation that Arendt either misperceived or missed entirely.

The Effects of Jim Crow on Black Families and Children

Protecting children is a crucial parental task and a primary obligation of adult society to children. At the same time, protection is not the only parental role. Philosopher Sara Ruddick argues that maternal practice encompasses a three-fold aim: the child's physical survival, the child's nurture and growth, and training of the child for successful participation in society. In a similar vein, David Blankenhorn attributes to fatherhood the tasks of providing, protecting, nurturing, and sponsoring/mentoring. As the adults primarily responsible for introducing their children to the larger world and their future roles in it, parents are called upon to perform complicated and evolving "liminal work," assisting their children at the boundaries between the family and the social and public world.

In the Jim Crow South, black families were routinely thwarted in their efforts to shield their children from the ravages of racism. Black children, exposed to a racially toxic white world, faced danger and the strong potential for hopelessness. For African American parents, the task of shoring up their children's sense of dignity and agency in a social world that impugned, undermined, and dismissed them was as daunting as it was crucial.

> "For African American parents, the task of shoring up their children's sense of dignity and agency . . . was as daunting as it was crucial.

The Jim Crow system of institutional and cultural racism inflicted a state of chronic, at times explicit, terror. Just as a lifetime of breathing contaminated air debilitates physical health, immersion in racist culture perpetrated and still perpetrates long-lasting harm on targeted individuals, families, and communities as well as on their white counterparts, although to different effect. The wonder is that the stories of southern black families were also narratives of survival, resistance, and courage; to the best of everyone's ability, local communities protected, nurtured, and trained black children for productive and dignified adulthood despite dehumanizing treatment by white society. But adult agency, including parents' roles as protectors, nurturers, and mentors of their children, was routinely undercut, often in public, humiliating ways.

Black authors' accounts of growing up in the Jim Crow South bristle with childhood memories of confusion, disillusionment, anger, and fear as the truths about their families' second-class citizenship, the punishment that could follow even minor transgressions of racial boundaries, and adults' inability to defend themselves or their children against race-based abuse became painfully clear. [Little Rock Nine student] Melba Pattillo Beals' memories of her parents being harassed by a local white storekeeper are representative.

Daddy was a tall man . . . with broad shoulders and big muscles in his arms. . . . Until that moment, I had thought he could take on the world, if he had to protect me. But watching him kowtow to the grocer made me know it wasn't so. It frightened me and made me think a lot about how, if I got into trouble with white people, the folks I counted on most in my life for protection couldn't help me at all. I was beginning to resign myself to the fact that white people were definitely in charge, and there was nothing we could do about it.

Beals remembers the hope and expectation that surged through the black community in the wake of the 1954 *Brown v. the Board of Education* decision. But *Brown* also sparked angry white backlash and, in the short run, more danger for black families. Shortly after the *Brown* decision, Beals, at age twelve, was sexually assaulted by a local white man who muttered about blacks forcing themselves into white schools. Her anguished parents did not report the assault for fear, she recalls, that "the police might do something worse to me" than she had already experienced. The brutal murder of fourteen-year-old Emmett Till in Money, Mississippi, in August 1955 was prompted by the Chicago boy's casual remark to a southern white woman and his boasting about having a white girlfriend. A widely acknowledged subtext for the furious southern white reaction to *Brown* and white opposition to the integration of Little Rock's Central High was fear that "forced racial mixing" would lead to interracial sexual relations and marriage.

> The decision of Little Rock's black teens and families to participate in integrating Central High was deliberate, clear-eyed about the risks, and gutsy.

In this highly volatile historical moment, the decision of Little Rock's black teens and families to participate in integrating Central High was deliberate, clear-eyed about the risks, and gutsy. The Nine's parents were well aware that their children were entering a dangerous situation and that there would be a price to pay by both children and adults. As Minniejean Brown Trickey put it later, "It was my father who lost his job. It was my mother who got the terror calls. It was my mother who was frightened for my life. [Our parents] were the heroes of this."

Civil rights leaders sought to employ this cruel fact—that black children were inevitably exposed to the degrading injustices that beset black adults—to positive effect. Although the most famous example was the 1963 Birmingham, Alabama, "Children's Crusade," where nearly one thousand schoolchildren were arrested in antisegregation demonstrations, southern civil rights campaigns regularly involved carefully considered, collective risk-taking by families and children. Fueling this risk-taking was the conviction among civil rights leaders that exerting strategic, nonviolent pressure on the strongholds of institutional racism could expose its perversity to public view, create support for legal redress, and thereby begin to undermine it. Despite real danger, movement families acted; in so doing, they bore witness to their hope in America's civic possibilities and to a courage nourished by Christian faith.

School Desegregation in Little Rock Yielded Mixed Results

US Commission on Civil Rights

In the following viewpoint, the staff of the US Commission on Civil Rights report on the state of school desegregation in Little Rock, Arkansas, twenty years after the Little Rock Nine crisis. The writers offer a history of desegregation beginning with the 1954 US Supreme Court decision in the case of *Brown v. Board of Education of Topeka*, a decision that overturned the "separate but equal" segregation doctrine. By 1977, according to the commission, reactions to desegregation are mixed. Black students find their conditions improved; some white parents are irked that their children must attend schools with black students.

Controversy regarding school desegregation in Little Rock has a long history. During the late 1950s, Central High School became one of the Nation's most notorious high schools. It was the example

---

SOURCE. United States Commission on Civil Rights, "School Desegregation in Little Rock Arkansas," June 1977.

segregationists used to argue that black and white students could never go to school together in peace. Violence in and around the school prompted President Eisenhower to dispatch Federal troops to Little Rock in order to keep the peace. Many of the scars of that desegregation effort are still present [in 1977] in Little Rock, yet many now feel the city has one of the most successfully desegregated school systems in the Nation. . . .

Desegregation in Little Rock

A Federal district court, acting on the basis of the 1954 Supreme Court *Brown* [*v. Board of Education of Topeka*] decision, ordered Little Rock to desegregate its public schools in 1957. The push for desegregation had been led by Daisy Bates (president of the Arkansas chapter of the NAACP) and diverse local groups such as the Black Ministerial Alliance, with the support of national organizations such as the Urban League and the NAACP Legal Defense and Educational Fund.

The initial effort to desegregate met with resistance from the community, the school board, and district administrators, and intervention by some State officials. This resistance was manifested in the eruption of trouble at Central High School. Wide publicity was given the dispatch of Federal troops by President Eisenhower to Central High to maintain order. The school district appealed the district court order, but simultaneously prepared a desegregation plan (called the "Blossom Plan" after school superintendent Virgil T. Blossom) for the 1958–59 school year.

The Supreme Court rejected the appeal in September 1958 in its landmark *Cooper v. Aaron* ruling ordering the desegregation of Central High School. However, the Blossom Plan was never implemented, for Governor Orval Faubus ordered the closing of Little Rock's public schools. The schools remained closed during the 1958–59 school year.

Schools reopened in 1959 under a pupil assignment desegregation plan, in which attendance zone lines were redrawn to enhance desegregation. This arrangement was kept until 1964, when the district instituted a "freedom of choice" plan allowing students in all grades to attend the school of their choice if space was available.

Beginning with the 1973–74 school year, all grades in the Little Rock schools were desegregated. Children from the east side were bused to 12 primary schools located in the west side of the city. Pupils in grades four and five in the west were bused to 10 intermediate schools in the east.

One additional change had been made at the high school level: In 1972 the students at Metropolitan High School were reassigned to one of the three present senior high schools so that that school could be converted into a center for vocational education serving all three school districts in Pulaski County. Little Rock students taking courses at this center were provided bus transportation.

The composite result of those actions was that enrollment at every school was almost equally divided between white and black students. Current [1977] school enrollment is approximately 52 percent black and 48 percent white.

The desegregation process was not only successful but extremely smooth, according to school and community observers. In comparison with other communities, there was little or no appreciable conflict. . . .

Parents' Response to Desegregation in 1976

In a series of Commission interviews conducted in February 1976, the most frequently mentioned concern of both white and black parents was busing. Neither white nor black parents wanted their children involved in the crosstown busing needed to implement the plan to create a unitary school system.

White parents, though concerned mostly with the busing issue, were also displeased that their children were compelled to attend interracial schools. There was general white parental hostility about completely desegregating the school system because many wanted to maintain the status quo at any cost. It was during the early 1970s that "white flight" occurred in Little Rock. Many white parents placed their children in private schools or in the Pulaski County School District (a separate district formed in 1927 by consolidating 40 rural districts).

> White parents . . . were also displeased that their children were compelled to attend interracial schools.

On the other hand, some white parents were pleased with the implementation of the plan for several reasons:

- The plan reduced the actual number of white students bused.

- Some white students were able to attend Hall or Parkview High Schools instead of Central, which is in the central city and had a predominantly black enrollment.

- The children, once transferred, continued through school with their companions and thus as a group did not break up.

- Some viewed the plan as improving the quality of education by reducing the size of classes, providing better instructional materials, and restructuring the school system.

Minority parents were also displeased with busing because a higher percentage of black students were bused than white: In the 1973–74 school year 58 percent of the students bused were black; in 1974–75, 56 percent of those bused were black; and in 1975–76, 57 percent of all students bused were black. However, there was a greater

RACIAL INTEGRATION IN SCHOOLS ON THE DECLINE

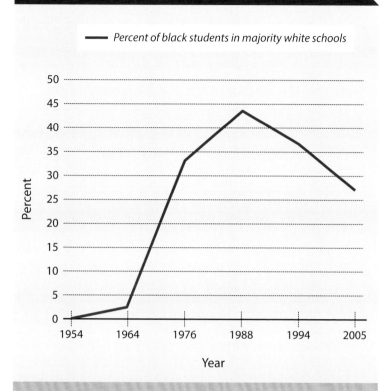

—— *Percent of black students in majority white schools*

Taken from: Gary Orfield, *Reviving the Goal of an Integrated Society: A 21st Century Challenge.* Los Angeles: The Civil Rights Project/Proyecto Derechos Civiles at UCLA, January 2009.

concern on the part of minority parents over the loss of neighborhood schools and the inordinate transfers of black faculty; for example, in 1972–73, of 314 teachers transferred, 54 percent were black. This percentage was disproportionately high because there were fewer blacks than whites in the school system at the time (315 black teachers out of a total of 1,065).

Generally, minority parents were pleased with the plan for the following reasons:

- Minority students went to better schools with better instructors and better instructional materials.

- Total desegregation was achieved within the school system.

- There was an equitable distribution of black faculty members.

Student Reactions to Desegregation

The reaction of the high school students interviewed was one of mixed emotions regarding desegregation. They expressed concern as to how they personally would be affected due to the desegregation process. Both black and white students cited violence in and around schools, apathy among black and white students, and discipline as the three most important problems faced by the district with regard to its students. Both black and white students also believed that the overall educational quality had increased for some students in Little Rock schools but had decreased for others. They cited a decline in the district average on national test scores as evidence of one negative effect desegregation has had on the quality of education. The white students believed that educational quality would continue to decrease, and, because some of their parents were strictly opposed to busing, the students themselves were contemplating attending private schools.

> Black students believed that . . . relations between the white and black communities had improved as had educational facilities.

On the positive side, the white students cited increased parental involvement in school affairs, better relationships between white and black students, the chance to meet different people, increased sensitivity, and improved educational facilities for blacks as side effects of desegregation. On the other hand, the black students believed that the opportunity for a better education for all students was attainable and that, indeed, relations between the white and black communities had improved as had educational facilities. In their opinion, the major negative outcome brought about by desegregation was "white flight" into the suburbs.

Teacher Response to Desegregation

Teachers' feelings about desegregation were mixed. In interviews with Commission staff, white teachers were generally pessimistic, and did not know if desegregation was necessary or if the plan would really work. Black teachers believed that desegregation was necessary. Both black and white teachers expressed their opinions, but neither group did anything actively to promote its views. The only participation that teachers had in the development of the final plan was through the local chapter of the National Education Association (NEA), which had limited involvement. However, individual faculty members were consulted about their transfers. Training in the areas of staff development and human relations was also provided for teachers after implementation of the plan. (During the first 2 years of desegregation, teacher-student relations were reportedly strained because of racial conflict.)

One positive change brought about by desegregation, according to those teachers interviewed, was the development of better relations between white and black students. On the other hand, there were some negative effects—for example, proportionately fewer black teachers than white ones were hired. This remained the case as recently as the 1975–76 school year, when approximately 52 percent of the students in the Little Rock School District were black, while the teaching staff was 29 percent black and 70 percent white. The involvement of the community leaders was seen by teachers as the single most important factor that initiated desegregation. White teachers thought parental opposition was the element that most impeded desegregation in the district, while black teachers frequently cited the closing of black schools.

White students of Little Rock's Horace Mann Junior High School, which was an all-African American school before desegregation, take a bus to school in December 1971. (© **AP Photo**.)

For the most part black teachers felt that the overall educational quality has definitely improved in the district. White teachers said that desegregation has tended to hinder white students academically, but that black students were definitely helped. White teachers said that test scores initially dropped, but are now improving because of the availability of better instructional materials and facilities. Black teachers said that more blacks are graduating from high school and obtaining jobs because of desegregation.

Administrative Thoughts on Desegregation

School administrators were not in agreement as to the desirability of desegregation prior to implementation in the district. One administrator was concerned about how the plan would affect the overall educational quality in the district. He was also concerned about white flight from central city schools.

All those administrators interviewed agreed that the superintendent and the board of directors were primarily responsible for the development of the plan because they had taken the initiative despite the lack of community support.

School administrators cited three factors as being extremely important in implementing desegregation in the Little Rock School District: superintendent leadership, the court orders which gave details on how desegregation would be accomplished, and the creation of a biracial committee of parents and staff. When the administrators were asked, "In your opinion, what specific educational changes or programs most facilitated school desegregation?" the general responses given were the elimination of overcrowded schools, human relations training, lower teacher-pupil ratios, inservice training, and staff development programs. Those factors that were cited as having impeded desegregation were "white flight," parental opposition, and community attitudes. . . .

> Factors that were cited as having impeded desegregation were 'white flight,' parental opposition, and community attitudes.

Public Reaction to Desegregation

Perhaps one of the most important steps taken by the district to desegregate its schools was the establishment of the biracial advisory committee to the school board in June 1973. The biracial committee made its first report to the board of directors in late April 1974. During the intervening months of work, it had deliberated on six areas of concern in school operations: cultural sensitivity in interracial relations, discipline, ability grouping, communications and public relations, instructional methods and processes, and the insufficient number of black personnel in the school administration.

Another effort to get more hands, hearts, and minds into the process of helping children to learn is the result of collaborative efforts of 18 community organizations. The primary coordinating body for this effort is Volunteers in Public Service (VIPS). This organization is funded locally by the Little Rock School District and other private organizations and individuals. The purpose of VIPS is to coordinate the use of volunteers throughout the schools. Community people who are willing to share their occupations, special hobbies, and travel experience are encouraged to become part of the VIPS special resource file. Volunteers work only in schools where their services have been requested. Among the many services they perform is an attendance calling service to make certain that children who are absent from school are at home or somewhere else known by the parents. Other volunteers present special topics in the classroom and tutor.

Despite this public participation in the schools, many Little Rock citizens fear that a widening gap exists between the schools and the larger community because of the continuing white middle-class flight to the suburbs. Some persons fear the loss of full participation in and support of public education. Others fear the emergence of an all-black school system. Despite these reservations, citizens have a strong faith in public education, and share at least in some degree the optimism about the future of the schools voiced by school officials. In general, all interviewees felt that there was evidence of some public interest and participation through community meetings and school visits by parents.

The Status of Desegregation in 1976 Little Rock

Desegregation efforts in Little Rock span 19 years. Extensive and involved efforts have been carried out by the courts, the school board, the NAACP and the NAACP Legal Defense and Educational Fund, and the citizens of Little Rock to achieve the goal of a unitary public school system open to all the children of the city regardless of race, color, or creed.

Instead of a comprehensive approach to desegregation, a variety of conflicting plans were introduced after the initial court decision. Some were rejected, and those accepted led to desegregation by segments or grades. This piecemeal desegregation was the strategy followed until the acceptance of a more comprehensive approach in 1973. At that time, the school district and the minority community agreed to work together toward bringing about complete desegregation of the schools.

The black community feels that throughout desegregation it has borne the largest share of the burden—for example, all-black rather than all-white schools were closed. White flight in the late 1960s has increased the degree of residential segregation in the city. Black administrators and teachers continue to complain that they receive unequal treatment and opportunity. Black parents dissatisfied with the unequal burden of busing have nonetheless accepted busing because it provides opportunities for their children to attend better schools.

There is a wide variance in community opinion on the merits of desegregation. The range is from open hostility and concern about the quality of the schools and education to positive assertions that desegregation has been of benefit to the schools and the city. The white majority has gradually accepted desegregation. Many persons interviewed believed that the efforts to facilitate peaceful desegregation were helpful but could have been more extensive.

> Although many problems still remain, the Little Rock School District has made good progress in desegregating its schools.

Despite the many conflicting opinions surrounding school desegregation in Little Rock, both the school administration and the various community organizations exercised positive leadership in bringing about desegregation. Although many problems still remain, the Little Rock School District has made good progress in desegregating its schools.

Racial Integration in Schools Is on the Decline Fifty Years Later

Juan Williams

In the following viewpoint, political analyst Juan Williams asserts that the United States has "lost its appetite" for school integration. He argues that segregation has been increasing since 1988. The consequences of the increased segregation, Williams states, is that more minority students fail to complete high school, thereby increasing the potential for poverty and unemployment in that demographic group. Williams uses the life successes of the Little Rock Nine as evidence for the benefits of integration. Williams is a political analyst for Fox News. He also writes for the *New York Times*, *Washington Post*, and *Wall Street Journal*.

F ifty years ago this week [September 27, 2007], President Dwight Eisenhower risked igniting the second U.S. civil war by sending 1,000 American soldiers into a Southern city. The troops, with bayonets at the end of their rifles, provided protection for nine black students trying to get into Little Rock's Central High School. Until the soldiers arrived, the black teenagers had been kept out by mobs and the Arkansas National Guard, in defiance of the Supreme Court's 1954 ruling ending school segregation.

The black children involved became the leading edge of a social experiment. Their lives offer answers to the question of what happens to black children who attend integrated schools, a question underscored by the recent Supreme Court ruling that voluntary school integration plans in Louisville and Seattle are unconstitutional.

The June [2007] decision said a focus on mixing students based on their skin color violates every student's right to be judged as an individual without regard to race. The ruling confirmed a political reality: America long ago lost its appetite for doing whatever it takes—busing, magnet schools, court orders—to integrate schools. The level of segregation in U.S. public schools has been growing since 1988, reversing the trend toward integration triggered by *Brown vs. Board of Education* [1954].

Schools Are Becoming More Segregated

The movement away from school integration is glaring. The Civil Rights Project found in 2003 that the nation's 27 biggest school districts were "overwhelmingly" segregated with black and Latino students. Nationwide today, almost half of black and Latino children are in schools where less than 10 percent of the students are white. Those essentially segregated schools have a large percentage of low-income families and, according to researchers, "difficulty retaining highly qualified teachers." Meanwhile, the average white

> Almost half of black and Latino children are in schools where less than 10 percent of the students are white.

Integration Benefits Racial Minorities

Studies over the past twenty years have demonstrated that integrated education leads not only to achievement gains in math and reading for African-American and Latino children, but also to increased occupational attainment, less involvement with the criminal justice system, and a greater tendency for graduates to live in integrated neighborhoods, have friends from many races and ethnic groups, and to be employed in diverse workplaces later in life.

SOURCE. *Philip Fegeler, "What We Know About School Integration, College Attendance, and the Reduction of Poverty," Spotlight on Poverty and Opportunity, April 5, 2010. www .spotlightonpoverty.org.*

student attends a school that is 80 percent white and far more affluent than the schools for minority students.

This trend toward isolation of poor and minority students has consequences—half of black and Latino students now drop out of high school.

Integrated schools benefit students, especially minorities. Research on the long-term outcomes of black and Latino students attending integrated schools indicates that those students "complete more years of education, earn higher degrees and major in more varied occupations than graduates of all-black schools."

That conclusion is reflected in the lives of the Little Rock Nine, who represent the black middle class that grew rapidly as better schools became open to black people during the 1960s and '70s.

Integration Benefitted the Little Rock Nine

Ernest Green, 65, who became the first black student to graduate from Central High, is the most prominent of the nine. He earned a master's degree in sociology and worked in the Carter and Clinton administrations. He is director of public finance in Washington for Lehman Brothers.

Melba Pattillo Beals, 65, chairs the African-American history department at Dominican University in River Forest, Ill., and wrote an award-winning book about her experiences at Central High; Elizabeth Eckford, 65, is a probation officer in Arkansas; Gloria Ray Karlmark, 64, moved to Sweden to work for IBM and later founded and edited the magazine *Computers in Industry*; Carlotta Walls LaNier, 64, started a real estate company in Colorado; Terrence Roberts, 65, is a psychologist in California; Jefferson Thomas, 64, fought in Vietnam and worked in government in Ohio for nearly 30 years; Minniejean Brown Trickey, 66, worked in the Clinton administration and is a visiting writer at Arkansas State University; and Thelma Mothershed Wair, 66, became a teacher.

> Part of [the Little Rock Nine's] success comes from their ability to mix easily with black and white people.

The Little Rock Nine and Interracial Relationships

Part of their success comes from their ability to mix easily with black and white people and to comfortably join the social and professional networks that segregation kept from black people. In fact, most of the nine worked in mostly white organizations. And four of the nine married white people (three black women married white men, and one black man married a white woman).

Ernest Green (center) was the first African American student to graduate from Little Rock's Central High School in May 1958. Some say that the ability to mix with white students helped the Little Rock Nine succeed in school and in their careers and that the same opportunity also helps other minority students do well in life. (© Grey Villet/Time & Life Pictures/Getty Images.)

In her book *Turn Away Thy Son*, Arkansas native Elizabeth Jacoway notes that the nine never take a group picture with white spouses or mixed-race children. Jacoway believes they don't want to take away from black pride in their achievement or reignite segregationist fears about interracial sex.

Terrence Roberts, who went on to become a psychology professor, thinks "fear of black people in the family" is still a driving force pulling Americans away from integrated schools. Ernest Green, whose first wife was white, calls it the "zipper issue . . . sex and race are highly combustible."

The interracial daughter of Minniejean Brown Trickey, Spirit Trickey, works as a Park Service tour guide at a memorial to the events at Central High. She says visitors regularly ask why so many of the nine broke the taboo against interracial marriage.

"My answer is that the Little Rock Nine followed the principles of nonviolence," she said. "They married who they fell in love with. But it is telling that so many people ask about it. It tells me where we are today."

A Controversial Museum at Central High School Depicts the Little Rock Nine Crisis of 1957

Johanna Miller Lewis

In the following viewpoint, University of Arkansas history professor Johanna Miller Lewis provides a first-person account of the research and work that went into the establishment of the Central High School Museum and Visitor Center commemorating the Little Rock Nine and the integration of public education. She argues that all stakeholders in the facility were surveyed, though not all chose to participate. According to Lewis, there were differing opinions about how the story should be told and whether such a museum should exist at all. Opened in time for the fortieth anniversary of the Little Rock Nine crisis, the museum has received generally positive response.

SOURCE. Johanna Miller Lewis, "'Build a Museum and They Will Come': The Creation of the Central High Museum and Visitor Center," *Public Historian*, vol. 22, no. 4, Autumn 2000. © 2000 by the National Council on Public History. Reprinted by permission of the University of California Press.

In September 1957, Arkansas Governor Orval Faubus defied the U.S. Supreme Court's decision in *Brown v. Board of Education* to end racial segregation in public education and used the Arkansas National Guard to prevent nine black teenagers from entering and de-segregating Little Rock's Central High School. After one aborted attempt to get the children into the school failed and a later attempt got them into the school but resulted in a riot outside (and the subsequent removal of the black students), President Dwight D. Eisenhower sent in the U.S. Army's 101st Airborne to escort the children into the school and counter Faubus's actions. Although black students remained enrolled at Central High School for the rest of the 1957–58 academic year, the following school year Governor Faubus closed the public high schools in Little Rock rather than continue with deseg-regation. If the events of fall 1957 hadn't done it, by this time the city had become a worldwide symbol of hate and intolerance.

Historical Questions Arise from the Crisis

What happened in Little Rock in September of 1957 raised numerous historical questions about the power of state law versus federal law, appropriate use of both the National Guard as well as the U.S. Army, and, of course, the president's ability to defend the Constitu-tion. For most Americans, however, the exact issues revolving around the crisis came a distant second to the explosive images of violence and hatred broadcast around the world through the new medium of televi-sion and the more traditional venue of newspapers and magazines. These images, some of which continually reappear in textbooks as well as histories and documen-taries of the civil rights movement, have now become ingrained in the nation's memory. The citizens of Little Rock have memories of the crisis that are not as fixed as a series of images, and they vary widely depending on their age, race, and involvement or proximity to the actual events.

The people of Little Rock and Arkansas struggled with the negative reputation created by these images for almost forty years. As the city gained a more positive media image as the home of President Bill Clinton, the time finally seemed appropriate to address the events of 1957 in a public manner. This [viewpoint] will discuss how the Central High Museum and Visitor Center was created quickly and with very few resources in time to open for the fortieth anniversary of the crisis.

Like many new museums, this project came with its own set of problems, including the difficulties of fundraising, opposition to resurrecting this negative incident, a local perception of the event that diverged sharply from the standard textbook portrayal of the crisis, and a tight timeline for completion. Unlike our "sister" museums, the Birmingham Civil Rights Institute and the National Civil Rights Museum in Memphis, which cover the entire civil rights movement in their exhibits (including segments on Central High), the exhibit at the Central High Museum and Visitor Center focuses solely on the '57 crisis and its origins and legacies, from an Arkansas perspective. . . .

Memories of the 1957 Crisis

Our two top priorities as an exhibit team became gathering archival photographs and television footage and devising a way to organize the research we had into an exhibit. At this point we looked to the community-based planning group to become our audience focus group and assist us in devising our message. These individuals continued to be quite forthcoming with their understanding of the crisis, and their expectations for the exhibit resulted in the emergence of a number of patterns that the exhibit team tried to follow.

1. Everyone had an opinion about what happened in 1957. Some believed that it was good for Civil Rights and the Constitution; others thought it was bad for public education. Locals wondered whether outsiders—anyone not from Arkansas who was not alive in '57—could truly understand what had happened in Little Rock. Most importantly, just about everyone agreed that the media coverage of this event was crucial.

2. The amount of passion people displayed about their ideas, and memories increased as they moved along a continuum from being alive in '57, a Southerner, an Arkansan, a resident of Little Rock, an adult resident of Little Rock, or a viewer/participant in the actual events.

3. Although people remembered that Faubus used the National Guard to prevent the Nine from entering the school and that Eisenhower called out the 101st Airborne to escort the Nine into Central High, few people were familiar with the details of the crisis. The little interest they expressed in knowing the facts was only surpassed by an outright hostility to what historians had written about the crisis, prompting one committee member to remark, "we don't care what the historians say."

Everyone Who Witnessed the Crisis Was Affected

Historical memory is powerful, especially when remembering one's own actions or reactions to a particular situation. In looking at the Central High desegregation crisis, the power of memory extends not only to the participants in the crisis—such as the Little Rock Nine, Governor Orval Faubus, Arkansas NAACP President Daisy Bates, or the white students at Central—but to *all* the people who witnessed the events, either in person or through the new medium of television. Unlike cold, hard, verifiable facts, historical memory is a melange of facts and opinions that frequently evokes emotions. For instance, the uncontrollable crowd that gathered outside of Central on September 23, the day the Little Rock Nine briefly entered the school, is a fact; exactly who was in the crowd—locals, out-of-towners, segregationists, or rednecks—depends on each person's memory. For instance, then-student Robin Woods later observed that "her school was surrounded by hoodlums." In fact, such memories are responsible for the citizens of Little Rock and Arkansas initially repressing the crisis as a painful episode in their history. However, mixed with time and a changing society, those same memories awakened a need in some Little Rock residents to deal with what happened in 1957 in a public manner. Whereas some citizens supported creating a museum or exhibit about the crisis as a way for people to experience their own personal catharsis about '57, others did so because they believed that a museum could publicly polish a city's otherwise tarnished racial legacy. . . .

> Some citizens supported creating a museum . . . because they believed that [it] could publicly polish a city's otherwise tarnished racial legacy.

The Museum Causes Controversy

Following a brief introduction to the topic under the title panel, "'All the World Is Watching Us': Little Rock and the 1957 Crisis," the first portion of the exhibit is subtitled "1776–1896: All Men are Created Equal?" By introducing the concept of equality as set forth in the Declaration of Independence, and discussing Arkansas, the Civil War, Reconstruction, and most importantly, the Thirteenth, Fourteenth, and Fifteenth amendments

to the Constitution, it sets the stage for some of the later legal issues of desegregation.

This portion of the exhibit also provided the first controversy that occurred in May 1997 and promptly landed on the editorial page of the Little Rock newspaper, the Arkansas *Democrat-Gazette*. In an effort to provide historical context for some 1958 photos taken of segregationists protesting with the Confederate battle flag and to enhance graphically the first section of the exhibit which dealt with the Civil War, we proposed hanging the Confederate battle flag next to a United States flag from around 1863. Stirring up some tension and trying to put the visitor on edge was another reason to have the flags in the exhibit. However, the "Stars and Bars" section created more tension among some of the board members than we anticipated. Two African-American board members and local politicians, Senator Bill Walker and Representative Irma Hunter Brown, persuasively argued

Displays at the Little Rock Central High School National Historic Site show information about the historic events related to school integration in Arkansas. (© AP Photo/ Danny Johnston.)

that having the actual flag in the beginning of the exhibit might make African Americans too angry to continue on to learn anything from the exhibit. A third African-American board member and member of the exhibit team, Ronnie Nichols, argued to keep the potent symbol, but the board voted not to include the flag in the exhibit. Although we removed the flags from this portion of the exhibit per the board decision, the 1958 photos that showed the Confederate flag remained in the exhibit. . . .

As mentioned earlier, the main emphasis of the exhibit became "1957–1958: A Time of Courage and Fear," because it is the academic year when the crisis occurred and that's what people associate with Central High. We handled the year with a powerful photo montage of evocative images diagonally cut through by a barricade (like the ones used by the police and the military) preventing the viewer from touching a blackboard, a symbol of education. To answer the all-important question of exactly what happened in the school, below the montage we placed an illustrated timeline of the entire school year detailing some of the harassment and violence directed at the Nine.

When we sent the exhibit script out for comment, this section garnered the most remarks. The Little Rock Nine were unanimous in their praise that after forty years of remaining silent, "their story" would finally be told. After the Visitor Center opened and they could see the actual design of the exhibit, many of them said that seeing the exhibit helped them realize that the pain they endured that year had, in fact, made a difference to others.

> The Little Rock Nine were unanimous in their praise that after forty years of remaining silent, 'their story' would finally be told.

The individuals whom we left out of the exhibit process, some of the white students at Central, had rebuffed early overtures to participate in the project. They were not quite as generous in their comments about the script. They accused us of writing a biased exhibit script, intending to make the students "look bad" by focusing on the "ugliness" of what happened and not the "95% of the white students who took no part in it." Instead, they wanted the exhibit to show more white students going about their daily business at Central. While we added a separate text panel, "The View from Inside the School," it did not detract from the Little Rock Nine's experiences. Even after the addition of the text panel, the constant refrain of these white students became "but we didn't do anything" to the Nine. . . .

Reactions to the Museum

Despite our claims that the exhibit served as a mere introduction to what happened in Little Rock in 1957, the local daily newspaper stated that the exhibit "imposed an artificial interpretation" on the crisis. Editorial writers at the *Arkansas Democrat-Gazette* believed that we left out important parts of the story, such as Orval Faubus's political foe, arch-segregationist Jim Johnson, and the vote taken in Little Rock in the fall of 1958 against immediate integration of all the public schools. Other publications have praised the Visitor Center and exhibit for bringing "1957 Little Rock to life" and illustrating "the horrors and hopes of the age." The Arkansas *Times* devoted an entire issue to the fortieth anniversary of the crisis, including the Visitor Center, and published the photograph of Elizabeth Eckford sitting on the bus bench with L.C. Bates. *Times* editor Max Brantley, a museum board member, wrote a surprisingly candid editorial describing how the Visitor Center came about, ending with the statement, "there's truth in all the conflicting emotions and views. And error. And distortions—honest and dishonest—of time, memory and context. Together, they are ample cause to face our past. With a new museum . . . we can't say we never had the chance to know better."

Arkansas State Senators Protest the Display of a Confederate Flag at the Central High School Museum

John Brummett

In the following viewpoint, *Arkansas Democrat-Gazette* columnist John Brummett reports on the opening of the Central High School Museum, set to coincide with the fortieth anniversary of the Little Rock Nine crisis. He comments on the protest by several African American state senators over the use of a Confederate flag in the exhibit, noting that historians want to include the flag for historical accuracy. He asserts that it is good that the issue has been settled quietly. He hopes that any controversy associated with the opening of the museum continues to be kept "under control."

SOURCE. John Brummett, "Flag Flap Settlement: Fight Was Ill Advised," *Arkansas Democrat-Gazette*, June 24, 1997, p. 7B. Copyright © 1997 by Arkansas Democrat-Gazette. All rights reserved. Reproduced by permission.

Some historians say that an effort to commemorate an event or an era with a museum should not be undertaken until a century has passed.

The point, frankly, would be to give everyone who lived through the event time to die. (Their kids ought to be getting on as well.) That should serve to weaken the innate defensiveness about reliving unpleasant history, not to mention the resentment-based arguments about what actually happened.

But there's another school of thought, more progressive if more perilous and painful. It is that sometimes it's important to confront recent history to move beyond it. So it is that we will not wait any hundred years to open a visitors center and museum in the old service station across from Little Rock Central High School. We will commemorate in the mid-lifetimes of most of the participants this epic event that qualified as a vanguard American incident in official white resistance to court-ordered racial desegregation of the schools.

We're only waiting until September, which will be the 40th anniversary of this internationally recognized affair from which Little Rock still reels. On this occasion, Little Rockians will be called on to come to terms with what happened and to reconcile with each other as

Several of the Little Rock Nine—including (left to right) Ernie Green, Gloria Ray Karlmark, and Carlotta Walls LaNier—sit with US president Bill Clinton and Central High student body president Fatima McKinra during ceremonies marking the fortieth anniversary of the desegregation of their high school. (© Joyce Naltchayan/AFP/Getty Images.)

The Controversial Confederate Flag

The familiar red flag with a star-studded blue diagonal cross was never the national flag of the Confederate States of America—it never flew over government buildings or other facilities. By the middle of the Civil War, however, it was the most visible Confederate battle flag pattern and had become the most important symbol of the fledgling nation. The blue St. Andrew's cross (or, more correctly, the saltire) on the red flag became in effect what it never technically was: *the* Confederate flag. . . . The era from the Civil War through World War II was a relatively coherent period of the flag's history, especially in contrast to the subsequent half-century. For those 85 years, the Confederate battle flag was the object of virtually uncontested public reverence in the South and increasing acceptance from the rest of the nation. Few people abused the flag, and few people complained openly about its public presence. Not coincidentally, African Americans were virtually excluded from the South's public life during most of those years. . . .

African Americans who lobbied unsuccessfully to remove the St. Andrew's cross from the Mississippi state flag tried to assure flag defenders that their agenda was limited. The president of the state NAACP testified that his organization wanted to change the state flag but was not out to erase other reminders of the Civil War. "There is no desire on the NAACP's part to go through the South tearing down Confederate monuments." On the other hand, he argued,

the state flag "flies over all Mississippi. It should represent everyone." Justice Fred Banks, Jr., the only African American on the Mississippi State Supreme Court, dissented from a 1998 decision allowing the battle flag to fly in displays along the state's Gulf Coast beaches. "I have no qualms with preserving history," he stated in his opinion. "Such symbols as the Confederate flag and the Nazi swastika are appropriate in museums, exhibits and the like. I do not believe, however, that it is appropriate public policy to continue to fly the Confederate battle flag at government facilities. To continue to do so under the shibboleth of 'preserving tradition' readily lends itself to connotations that, with good reason, offend a large number of Mississippi citizens—sending a message that their feelings do not matter."

Justice Banks's distinction between flags flying at government facilities and flags displayed in museums is a common argument in the flag debates. Flags flying at government facilities imply sovereignty and communicate symbolic messages of inclusion and exclusion that may have real consequences. Flags exhibited in museums are in an unambiguously historical context. These distinctions are often the basis of compromise, as many people honor the Confederate flag yet concede that state flags and state capitols are not the proper place for it.

SOURCE. *John M. Coski,* The Confederate Battle Flag. *Cambridge, MA: Harvard University Press, 2005, pp. 1, 272–273.*

a weeklong series of activities is held. A combination of city, state and private money has advanced the project to imminent completion.

As for the planning: So far, so good, I am happy to report.

A Flap over the Confederate Flag

The biggest flap among museum organizers has been whether to display a Confederate flag next to Old Glory in an opening display tracing the struggle for civil rights, and it's been settled quietly.

Two local black state legislators, Bill Walker and Irma Brown, objected. The Dixie flag sends all kinds of negative symbols to blacks, they said. They asked: Why burden the museum with a potential for racial battle reminiscent of what we've seen in Georgia and South Carolina?

Historical purists said that Walker and Brown had reacted precisely as people are supposed to react to honest and vivid portrayals in history museums—by showing that the display had served its purpose, which was to evoke emotion.

Both sides had a point. The historians had a stronger point generally. But in the specific case, a fight was ill-advised, especially when the Civil War is not the essence of the museum. And that was precisely the resolution. No Dixie flag.

Beyond that, official points of dispute have been of this variety: Why display a quote from Dr. Martin Luther King Jr. when, in fact, he had no role in Central High or the events leading to it? Why not a quote from Thurgood Marshall or Daisy Bates? Good point, and it properly prevailed.

> A seemingly inevitable undercurrent—local resentment by whites of the portrayal of themselves and their forebears as demons and thugs—[has] been evident.

That is not to say that a seemingly inevitable undercurrent—local resentment by whites of the portrayal of themselves and their forebears as demons and thugs—hasn't been evident. It's there. But it's been quiet, well under control, and we can hope it will remain so.

If there are those who think the museum will merely display a Tiger football helmet and jersey and a couple of '50s-vintage yearbooks, let them continue to think so. Then there is the missive that Rett Tucker, chief organizer of the visitor center and commemoration, keeps close lest his blood need to be set boiling. It is a returned fund-raising solicitation in which the recipient, remaining anonymous, returned it by marking that he would make no contribution, adding in red ink: "(This) is a disgraceful waste of taxpayer money. We ought to forget all about 1957 and how federal intervention destroyed a fine institution."

Central High today is a fine high school, especially for bright, fast-track students. It regularly leads the state, and competes on a national scale, in the number of national merit scholars it produces.

We have a calendar of events for Sept. 20–27 [1997] offering these highlights:—The actual museum opening at 10 A.M. Saturday, Sept. 20, with an open house at Central beginning at 11 A.M.—A weeklong exhibit at the state Capitol honoring Dunbar High School, the former black high school.—A 70th birthday party for the school at 1 P.M. Saturday, Sept. 27. The main event, with the time to be determined, will be held Thursday, Sept. 25, the anniversary date of the entry into the school of the nine black students under the protection of federal troops. President Clinton will attend. According to one report, the Little Rock Nine will walk into Central High as Clinton and Mike Huckabee—a former governor and the current one—hold open the door for them.

That ought to be quite a moment.

CHAPTER 3

Personal Narratives

Despite Army Protection, an African American Student Is Attacked

Terrence Roberts

In the following excerpt from his memoir, Terrence Roberts, one of the Little Rock Nine, tells that it takes the US Army to open Central High School to the African American students who have enrolled there. Despite the Army's constant presence and protection, Roberts was repeatedly harassed and attacked by white students. Roberts asserts that he avoided conflict as much as possible and relied on the training his mother gave him in nonviolence to withstand the onslaught. Roberts is a private practice psychologist and the CEO of a management-consulting firm.

Ultimately it took military force. President Eisenhower was forced to call in the 101st Airborne Division of the United States Army to open the

SOURCE. Terrence Roberts, *Lessons from Little Rock.* Little Rock, AR: Butler Center Books, 2009, pp. 108–114. Copyright © 2009 by Butler Center for Arkansas Studies. All rights reserved. Reproduced by permission.

school doors for us. The president was reluctant at first to take such action because he believed firmly in the concept of states' rights. It was his position that federal authority should be used sparingly, if at all, when disputes of this nature arose within the borders of a given state. Fortunately for us, there were people like Attorney General Herbert Brownell who urged the president to consider intervening. I understand also that [evangelist] Billy Graham and [singer] Paul Robeson, among other prominent U.S. citizens, spoke out about the need for protection for the nine of us.

Starting at Central High School

So President Eisenhower changed his mind. And on September 25, 1957, we entered Central High under the protection and guard of the 101st. It was one of the brighter moments of the whole experience. I felt relieved to know that whatever opposition we faced would be met by the force and might of the United States Army. This was a long-awaited and welcome statement that this country did indeed have a commitment to treating me with respect and ensuring that my basic rights were protected.

That morning the nine of us again assembled at the Bates home and piled into an army station wagon while machine-gun-mounted Jeeps patrolled the area. When we were ready to leave, the Jeeps took up positions in front of and behind the station wagon, and we formed a convoy that drove non-stop through the streets of Little Rock with sirens announcing our coming. Soldiers led the way as we stepped out of the station wagon and headed for the school's front door.

I felt very special at that moment. I was aware that something momentous was taking place. But years would pass before I would truly grasp the significance of what had happened. This was the first time since Reconstruction that federal troops had been ordered into the South to protect the rights of African Americans. On that morning, however, my primary thought was that maybe now I would not be killed for simply trying to go to school.

Soldiers in the School

For the first few weeks, the soldiers were present in great numbers, and one of them stood outside my classroom and walked with me from class to class. This was true for the other eight of us as well. All the soldiers of the 101st assigned to Central High were white. A command decision had been made about this on the assumption that the presence of black soldiers would be more provocative to the mob gathered around the school. I learned later that black soldiers in the 101st were eagerly looking forward to an opportunity to confront hostile white members of the mob and were more than disappointed to discover they would not be allowed to participate at Central. In retrospect the strategy probably was a good one. It is not likely that black soldiers would have been as restrained as their white counterparts, given the racially charged nature of the confrontation.

> This was the first time since Reconstruction that federal troops had been ordered into the South to protect the rights of African Americans.

We were only a few years younger than the soldiers, and I could read the lines of concern on their faces as the drama continued to unfold. Their job was made somewhat easier by the fact that several white students in each of my four classes got up, and after giving me the benefit of their best thinking about my ancestry, my skin color, my parentage, and also some unsolicited travel advice, walked out vowing never to return as long as I was there. "We will never be in school with n-----s!"

I am convinced that this group would have been the most troublesome had they remained in school. They were the ones who would have stopped at nothing to remove us from the school, dead or alive. Unfortunately, a large number of those who remained took on the responsibility of trying to drive us out of school. This group of students was willing to do whatever they could think of to persuade us to reconsider our decision to come to Central. They hit, kicked, pushed, shoved, slapped, tripped, scratched, spat on, and verbally abused us constantly.

They fell under close scrutiny of the 101st, and many times I was warned by my guard to avoid certain areas where trouble seemed to be brewing. When groups of

Dr. Terrence Roberts, a successful psychologist and retired professor, gives a speech at a ceremony honoring Martin Luther King Jr. in January 2007. (© **Phil Klein/Corbis.**)

students would gather in the more isolated parts of the school or when groups would hide behind bushes just outside exit doors, our guards would warn us. I was able to cope with a lot of the maltreatment because I believed that if things got really bad, the soldiers would just use their weapons and protect us with firepower. What I didn't know then, but discovered years later, was that none of the soldiers had ammunition. Another command decision had been made by General Edwin Walker to prohibit the use of loaded rifles at Central High. He feared a blood bath might ensue in the face of intense provocation. Since such an action would have been hard or virtually impossible to explain to the American public, he chose to use the threat of firepower rather than the real thing.

Choosing Nonviolence

In spite of the presence of the 101st, I had to contend daily with white students bent on causing me harm and injury. The nine of us had agreed to follow the principles of nonviolence although we had had only rudimentary training in this area. We had met with Dr. Martin Luther King, Jr., who came to Little Rock in 1957. And we had spent some time with Rev. James Lawson and Glenn Smiley, two men who had helped Dr. King refine his own understanding of nonviolence. But we were "winging it" to say the least. There was ample opportunity to practice, however, so we learned pretty quickly how to handle a variety of life-threatening situations. Jefferson Thomas says, for instance, that while he was dedicated to turning the other cheek, there was nothing in the rule book to suggest that he had to turn it in the near vicinity of his assailant. Jefferson reasoned that he could sprint to the other end of the hall and then turn the other cheek.

> I had to contend daily with white students bent on causing me harm and injury.

For some reason it had always been clear to me that the words spat out by the taunting students had actually very little to do with me. First, my mom had taught me that what others may say about me has nothing to do with me. Also, I had a lot of experience with this kind of thing from my junior high school days. There were some of my black classmates who had discovered that they could start fistfights by talking about each other's mothers. One would start the "dozens" with "Yo mama wears combat boots," or some other such nonsense. The dialogue would then escalate to the point where one would feel bested by the verbal prowess of the other, and the fight was on. My unwillingness to participate in the verbal jousting (and my fear of getting hurt in a fistfight) led me to develop a strategy that took the bite out of the demeaning (but often very creative!) remarks directed toward my mother.

I would say something like, "If you'd like, I'll take you home to meet my mother. She will be able to tell you whether your concerns about her footwear are right. You can ask her to her face if she owns any combat boots, and you can personally inspect her closets." This worked every time. Not one of them had the courage to take me up on the offer.

So when the white kids at Central tried to upset me with their verbal abuse, I was more than prepared. I concluded that they lacked the verbal skills necessary to play the "dozens." Although I never visibly reacted when confronted with the "dozens," I would think of great responses in my own mind and laugh to myself when I felt I would have won the exchange. I would say that my record was a winning one; after all, I had learned from the best practitioners.

One of the Little Rock Nine Discusses Life at Home and in School

Thelma Mothershed Wair

In the following viewpoint, one of the Little Rock Nine, Thelma Mothershed Wair, recalls several incidents from her days at Central High, including one in which she was accused of kicking a white girl and another when boys were throwing rock-laden snowballs at African American girls. She also recounts the response she received at home when she first mentioned her desire to attend Central High. Finally, she discusses what happened to her after she left Central High. Wair has worked in juvenile detention centers and as a counselor for homeless people.

We were American citizens who [paid] taxes and ha[d] the right to attend any public school. Central [had] a reputation for achieving academic excellence. Students who [did] well were offered scholarships to "top" colleges and universities. [The] faculty at Central was more diverse [and the] courses offered [exceeded] what was offered at Horace Mann, the black high school. Central offered Latin and German . . . Central was our neighborhood school. Most of the Nine could have walked to Central. We got to Mann on [a] city bus and even had to transfer!

Life Inside Central High in 1957–1958

After lunch one day, I was called to [Central High School vice principal] Mrs. Huckabee's office. When I entered the office, I saw a girl sitting and crying. I was told that she was crying because as we came upstairs from lunch, she said, "Thelma was in front of me, and kicked me." It was a complete lie. I told the girl, "If I kicked you, I apologize." That evening on the 6:00 news, her name was called saying that I had kicked her! . . . I was seated across from Minnijean Brown in the cafeteria when a white male student came and dumped a bowl of soup on her head. The 101st [Airborne] had left [the school]. . . . As I was going down a flight of steps to go home one day, someone on the landing above spat down on my poodle skirt. One day someone threw black ink on the back of my white blouse. . . . One day it snowed [and] Minnijean, Melba, and I were waiting inside a hall exit door for my mother to pick us up. The Arkansas National Guard were there to "keep peace." Some boys found small rocks and packed them into the snow and tossed them inside the hall at us. The Guards[men] said nothing to the boys, but ducked to keep from getting hit themselves! The guards[men] said nothing to the boys and when my mother arrived, as we ran to the car, the same foolishness continued.

In the mornings, students gathered for chapel, even though Central is a public school. Some of the Nine decided to attend Chapel since it was not spelled out as extracurricular. Chapel was a pleasant way to start the day with prayers, scripture, readings, and hymns. [It was] pleasant, until we looked around and found that some of the angels in the chapel were the same devils who gave us trouble in the hallways. . . . My homeroom teacher did not want to touch me. After being absent, we would go to the office to get a readmission slip for each teacher to sign. When I presented my slip to my teacher, she would look at me as if to say, "what do you want?" I would put the slip on her desk. She would sign it, place it in a book and slide it back over to me. I think she felt that if our fingers should happen to touch, she would suddenly turn into my color, up to her shoulders! Some kids asked us, "Why don't you go back to Africa?" My immediate thought was, "How can one go back to a place where [one] has never been?"

> Some kids asked us, 'Why don't you go back to Africa?' . . . . How can one go back to a place where [one] has never been?

Life at Home

When a notice came to [Horace] Mann that students interested in transferring to Central should sign up, several of my friends [did], and a lot more students signed up. When I got home, I told my mother what I had done. She was aggravated with me. She said, "How can you make it around that high place? Your heart might give out and then what would you do?" [Wair has had a heart condition since birth.] I told her that I was sure that Mann sent all my records, so they [Central] would read about my problem and arrange my schedule so that I would not have too far to walk. When my dad came home, they had a discussion and decided that I could attend, if I promised to drop Central if I became ill.

In the Little Rock telephone book were two listings for Mothershed—my family and a number for a white neighborhood. We occasionally got hostile telephone

In a 2007 photo, Thelma Mothershed Wair holds a picture of herself as a young woman. (© **Charles Ommanney/Getty Images.**)

calls at night. The caller would tell whoever answered the phone, "If you let that n----- come back to Central, we'll burn your house down." My brother, who is two and a half years younger than I, told them, "Come on—we've got something for you." We had nothing but kitchen knives! We decided that the way to protect our house was to not answer the phone. Our plan began to have whoever was last coming to bed, would leave the phone off the receiver.

Life After High School

I graduated "by mail" because Central was closed during my senior year. [I went to] Southern Illinois University at Carbondale, where I earned a Bachelor of Science

Degree in Home Economics Education. Southern Illinois University at Edwardsville is where I earned a Master's of Science in Guidance and Counseling. [I] taught Home Ec in a junior high. One day some girls came to me with their history book and said, "Ms. Wair, Mr. Reid said that you were in that Little Rock stuff. Were you?" There was a picture of the Nine climbing the steps to the school. I told them "Yes, I was in the Little Rock situation." I pointed to the picture, I said, "and there I am." One girl said, "In a history book, you sure must be old!" I told them, "Something historical happens every day." (I was 25-years old at the time!)

The mother of a student in Missouri wanted me to come to their school district and tell my story. She and her daughter came to pick me up and take me to a restaurant where they could quiz me and take pictures. A young woman working in the restaurant was an ex-student of mine. When I went to the ladies room, she asked them what the occasion was. When I came out, she asked me, "Ms. Wair, why didn't you tell your classes that you are famous?"

A White Central High Student Reports on the Situation at School

Beverly Maxine Burks

In the following viewpoint, the FBI interviews Beverly Maxine Burks, a white, fifteen-year-old tenth grader at Central High. Burks asserts that she has overheard older students discussing weapons and strategies for attacking African American students if they are allowed to enter the high school. In the second day of interviews, she adds that she circulated a petition calling for the removal of school superintendent Virgil Blossom and clarifies that none of the threats of violence were made before the National Guard was at the school.

SOURCE. Beverly Maxine Burks, "FBI Interview with Beverly Maxine Burks Regarding the Integration of Central High School, September 7 and 8, 1957," *Land of (Un)equal Opportunities: Documenting the Civil Rights Struggle in Arkansas*, Little Rock Central High Integration Crisis, Federal Bureau of Investigation Records (MC 1027), box 1. Special Collections, University of Arkansas Libraries, Fayetteville. Reproduced by permission.

On September 7, 1957, and September 8, 1957, Beverly Maxine Burks, [of] Little Rock, Arkansas, furnished the following signed statements:

I, Beverly Maxine Burks, furnish the following free and [voluntary] statement to Claburn T. White and Henry L. Tuck who have identified themselves as Special Agents of the FBI. This statement is being made in connection with an official investigation being conducted by the FBI, and I realize it can be used in a court of law.

I am 15 years of age and am a 10th grade student at Central High School, Little Rock, Arkansas.

On about September 4, 1957, before classes which commence at 8:45 A.M., I was in Pander's Drug Store located across the street from Central High School. There were numerous students in the drug store and also some boys that were not students.

I recall John Dix, an 11th grade student at Central High having a belt with some tacks or nails in it. Dix said the belt was to wrap around his fist and hit with the tacks or nails. He also had a switchblade knife.

Ronnie Muller, a 12th grade student at Central High showed a switchblade knife.

Dix and Muller said they keep the belt and knives in their lockers at school.

Don Duncan also known as Duncan, a 12th grade student at Central High, has a large pocket knife that I also saw on the morning of September 4, 1957.

Danny Johnson, who is not a student at Central High and whose address I do not know, keeps a tire tool in his car. I saw this tire tool in Danny's car Wednesday, Sept. 4, 1957. On this same day I also saw a tire tool in the car of Marion Gatrell, who is not a student and who I do not know the address. On September 6, 1957, I saw a tire tool in the car of Bill Johnson, who is not a student at Central High. Bill Johnson "said he would like to get hold of one of the Negroes to use what he has on him referring to the tire tool.

All of the above listed persons have stated in my presence they had the above weapons to use in case of trouble with the Negroes. Each has also said they would not start any trouble but if it did start they would be in the middle of it. They also said they had the weapons to protect themselves in the [event trouble] started.

> All of the above listed persons have stated in my presence that they had . . . weapons to use in case of trouble with the Negroes.

I do not know where any of these boys reside and have not seen any knives, guns, or any other type of weapons in possession of anyone else.

I have read the above statement consisting of this and two other pages and it is true and correct.

BEVERLY MAXINE BURKS

Witnesses:

CLABURN T. WHITE, Special Agent, FBI, Little Rock, Ark. 9/7/57.

HENRY L. TUCK, Special Agent, FBI, Little Rock, Ark. 9/7/57.

Beverly Burks' September 8, 1957 Statement

I, Beverly Maxine Burks, furnish the following free and voluntary statement to Claburn T. White and Henry L. Tuck who have identified themselves to me as Special Agents of the Federal Bureau of Investigation. This statement is being made in connection with an official investigation being conducted by the FBI, and I realize it can be used in a court of law.

I am 15 years of age and am a 10th grade student at

Central High School, Little Rock, Arkansas. I reside [in] Little Rock.

In [reference] to any knives, tire [tools] and weapons I have seen in possession of John Dix, Ronnie Muller, Don Duncan, Danny Johnson, and Bill Johnson, these weapons were all observed after the commencing of school on September 3, 1957. I did not see any knives, tire tools, or any other weapons in possession of the above persons or other individuals until after Sept. 3, 1957, and the National Guard was at the Central High School. I did not hear any remarks or discussion of violence toward the Negroes attending Central High School prior to September 3, 1957.

> I did not hear any remarks or discussion of violence toward the Negroes attending Central High School prior to September 3, 1957.

I do not recall that on September 6, 1957, or any other time at Ponder's Drug Store when Bill Johnson said anything about if they allow the Negroes to enter Central High School, we are going over to the school, pretend like we are students, and hide in the school, and if we catch a Negro walking down the hallway we are going to take him some place, and beat him up. I understand I was supposed to be present when Bill Johnson made this remark but I do not recall hearing this.

On September 4, 1957, I was given a petition to circulate among the crowd at Central High School. I was to obtain names on the petition and it was being circulated to obtain names for the purpose of removing Mr. Virgil Blossom and all of the school board members from office with the exception of Dr. Dale Alford. I obtained about 200 names on this petition. I mailed the petition to a Little Rock Post Office box number after I had finished obtaining names. I do not know the box number and do not know who gave me this petition.

After school on September 6, 1957, a Mr. Bickel contacted me at Central High School and wanted to know if I would talk to the FBI. I told him I guess so. I did not furnish any information to Mr. Bickel and had never seen him before. I had never furnished any information about seeing any type of weapons in possession of anyone or any remarks made by anyone concerning the Negroes entering Central High School prior to talking to Special Agents of the FBI on Sept. 7, 1957. No one had asked me about talking to anyone until I had talked to Mr. Bickel on September 6, 1957.

I do not know of any other incidents concerning Negroes entering Central High School of a violent nature or anything that has happened to cause violence.

I [have read] the above [statements consisting] of this and three other pages and it is true and correct.

BEVERLY MAXINE BURKS

Witnesses:

CLABURN T. WHITE, Special Agent, FBI, Little Rock, Ark., 9/8/57.

HENRY L. TUCK, Special Agent, FBI, Little Rock, Ark., 9/8/57.

The Long Shadow of Little Rock

Elizabeth Eckford, interviewed by Daisy Bates

The following viewpoint is excerpted from an interview between National Association for the Advancement of Colored People representative and journalist Daisy Bates and Elizabeth Eckford, a member of the Little Rock Nine. Eckford's experience on the day the Little Rock Nine attempted to enter Central High is highly traumatic; she was not informed that the group would enter the school together, and so she attempted to walk to school alone. Surrounded by a mob of angry white people, she was threatened with lynching. A photograph of Eckford with the mob surrounding her has become an iconic symbol of the Little Rock Nine crisis.

Elizabeth, whose dignity and control in the face of jeering mobsters had been filmed by television cameras and recorded in pictures flashed to newspapers over the world, had overnight become a national

SOURCE. Daisy Bates, excerpts from *The Long Shadow of Little Rock*. Copyright © 1962, 1986 by Daisy Bates. Reprinted with the permission of The Permissions Company, Inc., on behalf of the University of Arkansas Press, www.uapress.com.

heroine. During the next few days' newspaper reporters besieged her home, wanting to talk to her. The first day that her parents agreed she might come out of seclusion, she came to my house where the reporters awaited her. Elizabeth was very quiet, speaking only when spoken to. I took her to my bedroom to talk before I let the reporters see her. I asked how she felt now. Suddenly all her pent-up emotion flared.

"Why am I here?" she said, turning blazing eyes on me. "Why are you so interested in my welfare now? You didn't care enough to notify me of the change of plans—"

I walked over and reached out to her. Before she turned her back on me, I saw tears gathering in her eyes. My heart was breaking for this young girl who stood there trying to stifle her sobs. How could I explain that frantic early morning when at three o'clock my mind had gone on strike?

> I was awakened by the screams in [Elizabeth Eckford's] sleep, as she relived in her dreams the terrifying mob scenes.

In the ensuing weeks Elizabeth took part in all the activities of the nine—press conferences, attendance at court, studying with professors at nearby Philander Smith College. She was present, that is, but never really a part of things. The hurt had been too deep.

On the two nights she stayed at my home I was awakened by the screams in her sleep, as she relived in her dreams the terrifying mob scenes at Central. The only times Elizabeth showed real excitement were when Thurgood Marshall met the children and explained the meaning of what had happened in court. As he talked, she would listen raptly, a faint smile on her face. It was obvious he was her hero.

Little by little Elizabeth came out of her shell. Up to now she had never talked about what happened to her at Central. Once when we were alone in the downstairs

Civil rights leader and journalist Daisy Bates (center), an adviser to the Little Rock Nine, stands with four of the students in front of her home in September 1957. (© Thomas D. McAvoy/Time & Life Pictures/Getty Images.)

recreation room of my house, I asked her simply, "Elizabeth, do you think you can talk about it now?"

She remained quiet for a long time. Then she began to speak.

You remember the day before we were to go in, we met Superintendent Blossom at the school board office. He told us what the mob might say and do but he never told us we wouldn't have any protection. He told our parents not to come because he wouldn't be able to protect the children if they did.

That night I was so excited I couldn't sleep. The next morning I was about the first one up. While I was pressing my black and white dress—I had made it to wear on the first day of school—my little brother turned on the TV set. They started telling about a large crowd gathered at the school. The man on TV said he wondered if we were going to show up that morning. Mother called from the kitchen, where she was fixing breakfast, "Turn that TV off!" She was so upset and worried. I wanted to comfort her, so I said, "Mother, don't worry."

Dad was walking back and forth, from room to room, with a sad expression. He was chewing on his pipe and he had a cigar in his hand, but he didn't light either one. It would have been funny, only he was so nervous.

Before I left home Mother called us into the livingroom. She said we should have a word of prayer. Then I caught the bus and got off a block from the school. I saw a large crowd of people standing across the street from the soldiers guarding Central. As I walked on, the crowd suddenly got very quiet. Superintendent Blossom had told us to enter by the front door. I looked at all the people and thought, "Maybe I will be safer if I walk down the block to the front entrance behind the guards."

At the corner I tried to pass through the long line of guards around the school so as to enter the grounds behind them. One of the guards pointed across the street. So I pointed in the same direction and asked whether he meant for me to cross the street and walk down. He nodded "yes." So, I walked across the street conscious of the crowd that stood there, but they moved away from me.

For a moment all I could hear was the shuffling of their feet. Then someone shouted, "Here she comes, get ready!" I moved away from the crowd on the sidewalk and into the street. If the mob came at me I could then cross back over so the guards could protect me.

The crowd moved in closer and then began to follow me, calling me names. I still wasn't afraid. Just a little bit nervous. Then my knees started to shake all of a sudden and I wondered whether I could make it to the center entrance a block away. It was the longest block I ever walked in my whole life.

Even so, I still wasn't too scared because all the time

I kept thinking that the guards would protect me.

When I got right in front of the school, I went up to a guard again. But this time he just looked straight ahead and didn't move to let me pass him. I didn't know what to do. Then I looked and saw that the path leading to the front entrance was a little further ahead. So I walked until I was right in front of the path to the front door.

I stood looking at the school—it looked so big! Just then the guards let some white students go through.

The crowd was quiet. I guess they were waiting to see what was going to happen. When I was able to steady my knees, I walked up to the guard who had let the white students in. He too didn't move. When I tried to squeeze past him, he raised his bayonet and then the other guards closed in and they raised their bayonets.

> The crowd came toward me. They moved closer and closer. Somebody started yelling, 'Lynch her! Lynch her!'

They glared at me with a mean look and I was very frightened and didn't know what to do. I turned around and the crowd came toward me.

They moved closer and closer. Somebody started yelling, "Lynch her! Lynch her!"

I tried to see a friendly face somewhere in the mob—someone who maybe would help. I looked into the face of an old woman and it seemed a kind face, but when I looked at her again, she spat on me.

They came closer, shouting, "No n----- bitch is going to get in our school. Get out of here!"

I turned back to the guards but their faces told me I wouldn't get help from them. Then I looked down the block and saw a bench at the bus stop. I thought, "If I can only get there I will be safe." I don't know why the bench seemed a safe place to me, but I started walking toward it. I tried to close my mind to what they were shouting, and kept saying to myself, "If I can only make it to the bench I will be safe."

When I finally got there, I don't think I could have gone another step. I sat down and the mob crowded up and began shouting all over again. Someone hollered, "Drag her over to this tree! Let's take care of the n-----." Just then a white man sat down beside me, put his arm around me and patted my shoulder. He raised my chin and said, "Don't let them see you cry."

Then, a white lady—she was very nice—she came over to me on the bench. She spoke to me but I don't remember now what she said. She put me on the bus and sat next to me. She asked me my name and tried to talk to me but I don't think I answered. I can't remember much about the bus ride, but the next thing I remember I was standing in front of the School for the Blind, where Mother works.

I thought, "Maybe she isn't here. But she has to be here!" So I ran upstairs, and I think some teachers tried to talk to me, but I kept running until I reached Mother's classroom.

Mother was standing at the window with her head bowed, but she must have sensed I was there because she turned around. She looked as if she had been crying, and I wanted to tell her I was all right. But I couldn't speak. She put her arms around me and I cried.

Covering the Crisis

Will Counts

In the following viewpoint, *Arkansas Democrat* photographer Will Counts remembers the day he covered the story of the Little Rock Nine's attempted entry to Central High School. Counts describes his own background. He then tells how he came to snap a picture of Elizabeth Eckford—one of the Little Rock Nine—as she walked toward the high school and, close behind her, Hazel Bryan's face twisted with hate. (A different photo of the same event appears on page 12 of this book.) Counts's photo of the quiet African American girl and the white mob soon became the iconic image of the Little Rock Nine crisis.

As a news photographer I was preparing to record whatever happened at Central that morning of September 4th, but personally I desperately wanted the school's integration to go smoothly. I grew up believing in racial integration. In 1936, when I was

---

SOURCE. Will Counts, *A Life Is More than a Moment: The Desegregation of Little Rock's Central High.* Bloomington: Indiana University Press, 2007, pp. 29–34. Copyright © 2007 by Indiana University Press. All rights reserved. Reprinted with permission of Indiana University Press.

five, my farming parents had the opportunity to move to Plum Bayou, a Roosevelt administration resettlement community near England, Arkansas. While this federal project followed the state's segregation policies and only white share-cropper families were permitted to rent-to-own the Plum Bayou farms, there were always black families coming to help manually plant, cultivate, and harvest the crops. Here I began to know blacks, and my mother and father talked with blacks as friends. One of my fondest memories is of Lee Wilson, who I have always thought was my father's best friend. Mr. Wilson was a massive black man who made his living carrying railroad ties. He and my father would talk for hours, especially when my father was troubled. As an acknowledgment of the segregation mores, I was taught to call my dad's friend "Lee," not "Mr. Wilson," but I knew that he was a man to whom respect should be shown.

When World War II came, my dad went into military service, and my mother, brother, and I moved to Little Rock. Our neighborhood was racially mixed. While the city had institutional racial segregation, neighborhoods were not nearly so segregated as in many northern cities. There were often clusters of black families living in predominantly white neighborhoods. I grew up in such a lower-middle-class neighborhood, only a few blocks from the family home of Elizabeth Eckford, one of the Little Rock Nine. White and black kids played together on vacant lot playgrounds, and a black neighbor helped me with my first newspaper route. But when it was time to go to school in the fall, we suddenly became segregated. This never seemed right to me. Nor did it seem right to a number of my white neighborhood friends. Two of these friends, Milton and Claudia Davis, became strong civil rights activists when they volunteered to send their children to previously all-black public schools in Memphis.

Among the reporters and photographers covering the crisis at Central High, there was a spectrum of personal views on school integration. On the *Democrat* staff there were those who strongly supported Governor Faubus' segregationist stand, and there were those, like me, who were critical of his intervention into the desegregation process.

But we were united as a staff in trying to gather and report the news as accurately and fairly as possible. Working under editors Gene Harrington, Marcus George, and Bob McCord, I learned the professionalism of fair, accurate news reporting that was later the foundation of my journalism teaching. . . .

First Day at Central High

Governor Faubus' dramatic act in ordering National Guard troops to Little Rock Central High "to protect the peace" was the fire alarm for Little Rock's news media. Before that, I wasn't even scheduled to go to the school, but suddenly everything changed, and every available news photographer was assigned to the big story.

I carried only a Nikon S2 camera with a wide-angle lens. This 35 mm format camera was then rarely used by newspaper photographers, but the small camera gave me a substantial technical advantage over the other photographers, who were shooting with the then-standard 4" × 5" Speed Graphic press cameras. I was able to shoot thirty-six exposures without re-loading, while the others had to reload after each shot.

> In only my fourth month as a working photojournalist, I [worked] to capture on film the 'Decisive Moment,' that fraction of a second that would sum up the essence of the event.

In only my fourth month as a working photojournalist, I was trying to follow my idol, the French photographer Henri Cartier-Bresson. He believed that an event could best be photographed by shooting many exposures with the 35 mm camera, working to capture on film the "Decisive Moment," that fraction of a second that would sum up the essence of the event in both content and composition.

At the school on Wednesday, September 4, 1957, the news media didn't know where, or if, the black students would attempt to pass through the Arkansas National Guard troops. The massive school stretches for two blocks, between 14th and 16th along Park Street. For some unknown reason, newsmen started gathering near the 16th Street entrance, and quickly the media pack was clustered there.

As I was standing with this group of newsmen, George Douthit, an *Arkansas Democrat* reporter who covered the governor's office, advised me to go to 14th and Park streets. Douthit had gained the confidence of Governor Faubus and often had advance information about his plans. Some critics, even on the *Democrat* staff, would say that he had too close a personal relationship. I elected to leave the media pack and go to the corner as he had suggested.

There were only a couple of other newsmen waiting at 14th and Park when Elizabeth Eckford approached the National Guardsmen. White students had been passing through the line of troops along the sidewalk. I had suspicions but no real knowledge that the Guardsmen had orders to bar the black students from entering.

Divine guidance may have placed me in the best possible position to see and photograph Elizabeth Eckford as she approached the school. When she was turned away by the National Guard troops, the courage and grace she exhibited as she walked two blocks through the mob of school-integration dissidents became one of my most moving experiences. Her actions epitomized for me the nonviolent principles Dr. Martin Luther King Jr. and the Southern Christian Leadership Conference had begun using to compel the country toward racial justice.

But this 15-year-old girl wasn't part of the national civil rights movement. She has said that she wished to go to Central High school because she wanted to be a lawyer, and she believed that the excellent academic reputation and the wider course offerings at the school would help her toward that career goal. Before she became the first black student to attempt to enter Central High, Elizabeth had not met Daisy Bates, president of the Arkansas National Association for the Advancement of Colored People. She believes she was chosen by the Little Rock School District to be one of the Little Rock Nine because she wasn't tied to the NAACP.

Elizabeth's family was poor and didn't have a telephone in their home. Daisy Bates cites this as her reason for not informing Elizabeth of the plan for all the students to meet at the Bateses' home and go to Central High accompanied by a group of black and white ministers. Instead she came to school as instructed by the school's office, with the understanding that the National Guardsmen were there to protect her as she entered.

Her imperturbable walk through the mob has become a slow-motion *cinema verité* memory. I still find it difficult to believe that this display of racial hatred was happening in front of my high school and my camera.

As I watched and composed the photographs, I didn't know what might happen after each step Elizabeth took. The mob became increasingly strident, and while I saw no one attempt to strike Elizabeth, that possibility was always present. The National Guard troops remained on the sidewalk, passively watching the crowd verbally assail her. It was only as she neared the bus stop at 16th and Park streets that a National Guard officer briefly moved into the crush of demonstrators.

> I still find it difficult to believe that this display of racial hatred was happening in front of my high school and my camera.

Elizabeth has told me that as she was sitting on a bench at the bus stop, she wondered why the newsmen, including me, who crowded around didn't assist her onto a bus. I have no good answer for her question.

An Expelled Little Rock Nine Student Remembers the Little Rock Crisis

Minnijean Brown Trickey, interviewed by Elizabeth Jacoway

In the following viewpoint, author Elizabeth Jacoway interviews Minnijean Brown Trickey, the Little Rock Nine student who was expelled from Central High School after being accused of spilling chili on a group of white boys and calling a girl "white trash." Brown offers her recollection of these events and takes issue with the characterization of her given by Central High vice principal Elizabeth Huckaby in her memoir. She also discusses the philosophy of nonviolent protest and states that she feels sorrow more than anger over the events surrounding the crisis. Now retired, Trickey served as deputy assistant secretary of the Department of the Interior under President Bill Clinton.

SOURCE. Minnijean Brown Trickey, interviewed by Elizabeth Jacoway, "Not Anger, But Sorrow: Minnijean Brown Trickey Remembers the Little Rock Crisis," *Arkansas Historical Quarterly*, vol. 64, no. 1, Spring 2005, pp. 1–26. Copyright © 2005 by Arkansas Historical Association. All rights reserved. Reproduced by permission.

Minnijean Brown: . . . The worst thing that ever happened to me at Central after the 101st [Airborne] left, and the parents were carpooling, and I was coming out the side door. My mom was sitting in a car, and as I walked this guy came and kicked me down the steps. The part that was the worst was that my mother saw it. She, of course, went into the school, and I kept saying, "Don't go in there because they are not going to listen to you." I didn't want her to be hurt by going in and trying to present this and having them treat her like they treated us—"You're just so excitable. Now are you sure that happened and do you know his name? Do you know her name? Did a teacher see it? Well, you know, I don't think there is anything we can do if no one saw it." I just didn't want that to happen to her.

Elizabeth Jacoway: So you didn't let her go in?

Well, she did go in, and she also tried to have him charged with assault, but they wouldn't accept it at the police department. That's why I get so mad. I read a line in [Central High School vice principal] Mrs. [Elizabeth] Huckaby's book: "Minnijean was so volatile." I wasn't volatile. Hell, stuff was being done to me every day that will never be recorded in anybody's annals, and I'm the one who was volatile? Isn't that interesting?

The Brown Family Is Mistreated

What was some of the stuff that was being done to you?

Well, the main thing that was being done to me was that after I dropped the chili, well my dad didn't get any work and the phone was ringing all night. People were throwing rocks through my window and squeaking their driving through the middle of the night, burning rubber, and yelling obscenities. My little brother, we tried to keep him from answering the phone. We'd take the phone off the hook at night. But you're having just call after call after call after call, and first you just hang up, and then you're just so livid because it's a total form of terror, just constant. And then there was the thing of not being able to go anyplace. The way it was, you were forced to be inside. You couldn't go anyplace. If I went downtown, people would line up and go [whisper sound] hee, hee, hee, hee. You just didn't go. You were kind of trapped.

Well, I'll tell you the name of the person who befriended me. Her name was Mary Ann Rath.

Her father was on the school board.

I didn't know that, but she would actually walk beside me.

Wow.

And I haven't been able to thank her.

The white girl who befriended Elizabeth Eckford was Ann Williams. I'll tell you someone else whose name comes up as one of the white girls who befriended you all, who was a friend of Mary Ann Rath, is Marietta Meyer.

The name sounds familiar.

Her father owned Meyer's Bread.

The Kindness of Strangers

Okay and the other thing that I think I need to tell you—because I'm really in the process of trying to talk about people who helped—is that when I got to go to New York somebody called my mother and said: "I own a dress store. Come and let her get what she needs." They gave me a cashmere coat and a suit. They said, "Anything you want, you try on and you can have."

Oh my goodness. Do you remember who that was?

I don't know the name of the store. Now I don't know if somebody else paid for it and said do it, or whether they did it because. . . . You couldn't tell, because that's the nature of the separation under segregation. You don't even know where the source of anything is.

When it came to the segregationists and the violence, you know everybody says all those people out there were from out of town, but they weren't.

A lot were that were in the mob on September 23rd, but the kids in the school who tormented you all were not from out of town.

Chris Mercer [field secretary for the National Association for the Advancement of Colored People] needs more recognition because he was a young person with a commitment. He just did all the running around and driving and all kinds of stuff. I mean Daisy [Bates, civil rights activist] was kind of imperious. She liked to tell people to do this, do that, do this at the point when she became such a heroine, you know at the point that she became the center of it. One of the things is to not let the images and the stories again tell me what happened. And that's why it's so hard to get to it because there are all these versions and I'm not sure which is the real one. . . .

Combating Conflicting Truths

And so many of the truths are in conflict.

That's okay. That's the nature of life, and it can be in conflict, and then people draw their own conclusions. You know, that's the challenge I give to kids. Don't listen to all that. Read a whole bunch of versions so that you know that it's inexact, and then you can kind of figure it out from that. Don't be fully persuaded by any perspective because that's not what a thinking person does. So, yeah, I think we can handle various truths. The official record says that I got expelled,

> The official record says that I got expelled, that I called these girls white trash. . . . But it wasn't that way.

that I called these girls white trash, and then they hit me with the purse full of combination locks. But it wasn't that way. And [Little Rock school superintendent] Virgil Blossom went to his death knowing it was a lie, and so did Elizabeth Huckaby. They know that it didn't happen that way—that I called them a name and then they hit me with the purse. But it's on my expulsion record. So I said, "I know you are not going to change this because this is the official record, but that is not the truth." And when I think about it now that I'm older, my teacher didn't come out when they were calling me names and standing there pushing me against the wall, and she didn't see the purse when it hit me on the back of the head. She saw it when I picked it up, decided what to do with it, dropped it again, and said, "Leave me alone, white trash." She saw that, but she didn't see the whole two weeks before when they followed me from the door to the third floor to my homeroom. And so now that I'm older and see how much conspiracy and how much lies and how much horribleness we do to justify bombing somebody or whatever, I'm starting to think that it was designed. You know Elizabeth Huckaby says "so volatile," but maybe that was a design to actually push me against the wall until I did respond.

> I think that I was a saint that they didn't get a response out of me before they did.

I imagine it was. Because they had targeted you. They thought they could get a response out of you.

Well, I think that I was a saint that they didn't get a response out of me before they did and a superhuman. The other part to me—okay, this is a point that I think is really important. The way they framed me as being this volatile person means that I was really stupid, and I'm in a situation of 2,000 to 9, and I'm going to be that volatile, and I'm going to be talking back, and I'm going to be saying things. To me, it's the ultimate, ultimate put-down, because it says, "She's so stupid that she's going to be acting like a crazy person with these odds, in all this danger." Do I look like I'm that stupid? And so my daughter came home, and she said, "Did you actually push this white guy and say 'Get out of my way white boy'?" I said, "Think about it [laughs]. In your wildest imaginings of me being stark raving nuts, is that the kind of thing I would do?" And would I do it in light of the fact that the whole world is watching me, the National Guard is watching me, all the kids are watching me. Am I so stupid? So to me that's why it's so frustrating, because it assumes that I was so stupid that I was constantly walking around picking fights. Their idea of breaking me was to get me to talk back, but my idea of them breaking me was to make me cry or to make me finally put my head down. I didn't realize that their breaking of me was to make me say something, but they would have taken me bursting into tears, they would have taken me staying at home, they would have taken anything. Their idea of breaking me was to get me to say something, and I thought they were trying to get me to cry. Most of the time I was wanting to hold myself together because the fear that I had would be that I would just explode and my body would just splatter on the walls of Central and on that marble floor and all that.

Holding It Together

So my energy was not really about responding to them. We didn't have the energy to respond to them. We were busy holding ourselves together intact and not just go screaming out the door. So that's why I'm so [angry] about the way I've been described. The effort that it required just to be in there wasn't—you couldn't even imagine having anything to respond with. To be able to open your mouth in a class when they are all like "hee, hee," and you are just, like, "I can talk, I'm capable of speaking, and I will speak very clearly, and I will try not to have one of those disgusting southern accents the way they did." So our resistance was a lot more sophisticated than a response to them. And we don't want to be them. We didn't want to be like them. We didn't want to be crude and gross. We wanted to get them in another way. We wanted to be smarter than they were and show that we were smarter than they were. So I mean resistance is a weird thing. How do you resist if nobody tells you how to resist? Well, somebody did, [nonviolence advocate and Martin Luther King Jr. ally] James Lawson, who had been in India, did tell us.

At what stage of the process?

Really early. The nature of nonviolent resistance. It wasn't a deep long thing. Daisy apparently doesn't talk about it. Ernie knows about it.

But he came and met with the nine?

Yes.

I wonder who set that up.

Maybe he set it up. You know, maybe Dr. King set it up. Maybe he felt he needed to. [Lawson] was actually in India in the early '50s and hung out in the Gandhi movement.

Dropping the Chili

So the other part of my so-called "volatility" was that I also knew some strategies, and the strategy was never to answer back. I dropped the chili. I didn't dump a bowl of chili. I dropped the tray, the bun, the milk, the fork, the straw, all of it. I just opened my hand like that.

Oh, really, you didn't dump it over [the boy's head]?

Oh no, no. It was kind of like when I went through once and then I went back because I was nonviolent. Okay, I was going [to] do my nonviolence training. The smart thing would have been to just go to another place, but one of the things that was true about Central is if this group was bugging me, there were other groups. It was all planned, right. It was like the girls were doing their part of snickering and [saying] things [like] "Look what she's got on" and all this. But one of the guys, the guys who got, actually four guys got splattered with chili.

One of them is Dent Gitchel. He's a lawyer here.

Okay, he didn't do anything.

Right.

The other guys on the other side were kicking his chair.

Mrs. Huckaby says in her book that he came in looking really sheepish with this other guy—I've forgotten his name—and they were both covered you know with soup or whatever. She said he was a nice guy, and she couldn't believe he did that, and he said "Mrs. Huckaby, Minnijean did not mean to do this. In fact, I don't know how she has put up with this as long as she has."

Well, [long pause before bursting into tears] I didn't read her book because I didn't want to hear all that shit. But I need to hear this because I just feel like "Oh God. He did, he apologized," and I mean he did, but it was still like nobody heard him. Nobody heard what he said. It was like their ideas of who I was were so powerful that they couldn't even hear their own kids. I've never forgotten him because I've tried to remember those people who were kind in some really subtle way, and I've tried to be kind for my whole life because I know that maybe nobody is ever going to say to you that you were kind. But they are going to take it into the deepest part of their heart, and it's going to have so much meaning, and you don't really ever know. You don't really know. . . .

Where that energy is going to end up?

Yes, you don't know how important it's going to be to somebody. I'm sorry. I don't mean to cry but I hate— that's what I mean about it. It's like, hard. I just really, really, really have a hard time. I don't know how you heal from it. I really don't. I just stayed anonymous just about most of my life. I don't tell anybody anything about that because I want to be accounted for and accountable to myself and I don't want to have to have that determining. My strongest emotion—I always thought it might be anger—but my strongest emotion turned out to be sorrow. So I know I'm not that person they said I was.

> My strongest emotion turned out to be sorrow. So I know I'm not the person they said I was.

CHRONOLOGY

1949   September: University of Arkansas School of Law is the first public institute of higher education to be integrated.

1954   May 17: The US Supreme Court rules on the *Brown v. Board of Education of Topeka* case, stating that segregation by race is unconstitutional in public schools. The ruling opens the door for desegregation of the nation's thousands of racially segregated schools.

1955   May 24: The Little Rock school board agrees that integration at the high school level will begin in two years, and that younger students will be integrated gradually over a period of six years.

1956   January 23: A group of African American students attempt to enroll in Little Rock white schools, but are denied.

February 8: The National Association for the Advancement of Colored People (NAACP) sues the Little Rock schools on behalf of African American students. The suit is later dismissed on the grounds that the Little Rock School Board had a plan for more gradual integration. The NAACP appeals, but the dismissal is upheld in April 1957.

1957   Spring: The process of desegregating Little Rock Central High School begins with interviews of eighty African American students who wanted to attend the school. The superintendent selects seventeen of these students; only nine complete the process for enrolling at Central.

Summer: Little Rock citizens opposed to desegregation form the Capital Citizens Council and the Mother's League of Central High School.

September 2: Governor Orval Faubus calls out the Arkansas National Guard to promote peace on the first day of school at Central High.

September 4: Nine African American students attempt to enter Central High but are prevented from doing so by the National Guard.

September 9: Judge Ronald Davies of the US District Court for the Eastern District of Arkansas begins injunction proceedings against Faubus and two National Guardsmen for preventing the integration of Central High.

September 14: Faubus meets with President Dwight D. Eisenhower in Newport, Rhode Island.

September 20: The Little Rock Nine enter Central High through a side door to avoid the more than one thousand protestors in front of the school. A riot ensues, and Little Rock police escort the African American students out of the school.

September 24: President Eisenhower sends the 101st Airborne Division of the US Army to Little Rock.

September 25: The Little Rock Nine enter Central High under Army protection.

1958   May 8: Eisenhower removes the federalized National Guard from Central High School.

May 27: Little Rock Nine student Ernest Green graduates from Central High, the first black student ever to do so.

August: The Arkansas State Legislature passes a law allowing the governor to close public schools to avoid integration and to lease the closed schools to private corporations.

September 27: Voters overwhelming oppose integration by a vote of 7,561 in favor and 129,470 opposed. Public high schools in Little Rock are closed for the year.

1959   June: A federal judge rules Faubus's actions unconstitutional and orders him to reopen the schools.

August: School resumes with African American students attending both Central and Hall high schools.

1972   Fall: All grades in Little Rock public schools achieve racial integration.

1982   May 20: Central High School is designated as a National Historic Site.

1987   October 24: All members of the Little Rock Nine return to celebrate the thirty-year anniversary of the integration of Central High School.

1999   November 9: Members of the Little Rock Nine receive the Congressional Gold Medal.

2007   September 24: A museum honoring the Little Rock Nine opens, fifty years after the initial crisis.

FOR FURTHER READING

Books

Herb Boyd, *We Shall Overcome*. Naperville, IL: Sourcebooks, 2004.

Clare Cushman and Melvin I. Urofsky, eds., *Black, White, and Brown: The Landmark School Desegregation Case in Retrospect*. Washington, DC: CQ, 2004.

Judith Bloom Fradin and Dennis B. Fradin, *Daisy Bates and the Little Rock Nine*. New York: Clarion, 2004.

Erica Frankenberg, Gary Orfield, and Paula D. McClain, eds., *Lessons in Integration: Realizing the Promise of Racial Diversity in American Schools*. Charlottesville: University of Virginia Press, 2007.

Tony A. Freyer, *Little Rock on Trial: Cooper v. Aaron and School Desegregation*. Lawrence: University Press of Kansas, 2007.

Peter H. Irons, *Jim Crow's Children: The Broken Promise of the Brown Decision*. New York: Viking, 2002.

Jonathan Kozol, *The Shame of the Nation: The Restoration of Apartheid Schooling in America*. New York: Crown, 2005.

Kekla Magoon, *Today the World Is Watching You: The Little Rock Nine and the Fight for School Integration, 1957*. Minneapolis: Twenty-First Century Books, 2011.

David Margolick, *Elizabeth and Hazel: Two Women of Little Rock*. New Haven, CT: Yale University Press, 2011.

Mara Miller, *School Desegregation and the Story of the Little Rock Nine*. Berkeley Heights, NJ: Enslow, 2008.

Charles J. Ogletree, *All Deliberate Speed: Reflections on the First Half Century of Brown v. Board of Education*. New York: W.W. Norton, 2004.

Gary Orfield and Susan Eaton, *Dismantling Desegregation: The Quiet Reversal of Brown v. Board of Education.* New York: New Press, 1996.

James T. Patterson, *Brown v. Board of Education: A Civil Rights Milestone and Its Troubled Legacy.* Oxford, England: Oxford University Press, 2001.

Terrence J. Roberts, *Simple, Not Easy: Reflections on Community, Social Responsibility and Tolerance.* Little Rock, AR: Parkhurst Brothers, 2010.

Juan Williams, *Eyes on the Prize: America's Civil Rights Years, 1954–1965.* New York: Penguin, 2002.

Mitch Yamasaki, *Civil Rights Movement, 1954–1968: We Shall Overcome, Some Day.* Boston: History Compass, 2007.

Periodicals

Regina Agoha, "Little Rock Remembers: Little Rock Nine," *Air Mobility Command*, February 23, 2012. www.amc.af.mil.

Lerone Bennett Jr., "Chronicles of Black Courage: The Little Rock 10," *Ebony*, vol. 53, no. 2, December 1997, pp. 132–140.

Kevin Boyle, "What a Forced Friendship Can't Erase," *Washington Post*, October 23, 2011, p. B01.

Robert L. Brown, "The Third Little Rock Crisis," *Arkansas Historical Quarterly*, vol. 65, no. 1, Spring 2006, pp. 39–44.

John Brummett, "Bill Walker's Version: The Rebel Flag and Other Things," *Arkansas Democrat-Gazette*, May 17, 1997, p. 11B.

Ed Caesar, "Captured in Black and White; a Racist Slur, Caught on Camera in Arkansas in 1957," *Sunday Times*, October 30, 2011, p. 48.

William Clinton, "Speech: 50th Anniversary Commemoration of Central High School," Clinton Foundation, September 25, 2007. www.clintonfoundation.org.

Ellis Cose, "Little Rock, 50 Years Later," *Newsweek*, vol. 150, no. 13, September 24, 2007, p. 41.

"Desegregation: Diversity Remains Elusive: Recent Supreme Court Ruling Highlights Key Issues Under Debate Today," *Reading Today*, vol. 25, no. 1, 2007, pp. 1–2.

Jonathan Guryan, "Desegregation and Black Dropout Rates," *American Economic Review*, vol. 94, no. 4, September 2004, pp. 919–943.

Carrie Kilman, "Gates of Change," *Teaching Tolerance*, no. 31, Spring 2007, pp. 44–51.

"Little Rock: 40 Years Later," *New York Times Learning Network*, 1997. tv.nytimes.com.

David Margolick, "Elizabeth Eckford and Hazel Bryan: The Story Behind the Photograph That Shamed America," *The Telegraph*, October 9, 2011. www.telegraph.co.uk.

Lonnae O'Neal Parker, "Legacy of Courage," *Detroit News*, February 16, 2012, p. B1.

Melba Pattillo Beals, "Beyond Racism: A 'Little Rock Nine' Member and Civil Rights," *Christian Science Monitor*, September 18, 2010. www.csmonitor.com.

Homer Rigart, "Faubus Sees 'Occupation'; Tension at School Eases; President Sets a Parley," *New York Times*, September 27, 1957.

Shea Steward, "What White Flight? Little Rock Schools Remain More Diverse than Those in Other Southern Cities," *Sync Weekly: Arkansas Democrat-Gazette*, September 18, 2007. www.syncweekly.com.

Andrea Stone, "In Little Rock Nine, a Small Act of Defiance," *USA Today*, August 30, 2007. usatoday30.usatoday.com.

Susan Ulbrich, "Students Learn About Integration," *Daily News* (Jacksonville, NC), February 28, 2011.

Nancy Van Valkenburg, "Little Rock Nine Student's Message: Invest in Yourself," *Standard-Examiner*, February 15, 2012. www.standard.net.

Joanna Walters, "'Little Rock Nine' Prepare to Celebrate Day of Victory: The President-Elect Has Invited as Inauguration

Guests the Nine Black People Who as Children Defied Racist Mobs in Arkansas over 50 Years Ago," *The Observer*, December 28, 2008, p. 30.

Websites

Little Rock Nine Foundation (www.littlerock9.com). This website provides students with information about the Little Rock Nine, including biographies and a historical summary of the event. Included are current photographs of the Little Rock Nine and press releases about them.

National Park Service: Little Rock Central High School (www.nps.gov/chsc). Little Rock Central High School is a National Historic Site administered by the National Park Service, which maintains this website. The site has information for planning a visit to Central High, documents and photographs, brochures, historical and cultural summaries, and news releases. Teachers can also access lesson plans and teaching materials.

University of Arkansas: Land of (Unequal) Opportunity: Documenting the Civil Rights Struggle in Arkansas (http://digitalcollections.uark.edu/cdm/landingpage/collection/Civil rights). This website from the University of Arkansas Library's digital collection includes analysis, summaries, and primary text documents such as speeches, FBI interviews, photographs, and articles on the Little Rock school desegregation crisis.

INDEX